FOOD

RETAIL DESIGN & DISPLAY 2

FOOD
RETAIL DESIGN & DISPLAY 2

Edited by Martin M. Pegler, SVM

RETAIL REPORTING CORPORATION • NEW YORK

Retail Reporting Corporation
302 Fifth Avenue
New York, NY 10001

Distributors to the trade in the United States and Canada
Van Nostrand Reinhold
115 Fifth Avenue
New York, NY 10003

Distributed outside the United States and Canada
Hearst Books International
1350 Avenue of the Americas
New York, NY 10019

Library of Congress Cataloging in Publication Data:
Food Retail Design & Display / 2

Printed and Bound in Hong Kong
ISBN 0-934590-51-6

Designed by Bernard Schleifer

CONTENTS

In the political area, this year, we are hearing sound bytes about "family values" and "traditions" — a return to "the good old ways." If anything, from a retail point of view, the '90s will also be a return to "values" and "traditions" and though fashions are always supposed to be new — they too are often based on styles or motifs of the past. Thus there is everywhere the recurring theme of "return to the past." In getting the material for this edition of Food Retail Design & Display, I researched what was "new" — who was doing what — and where things were happening. I did not have any preconceived notions or even an "agenda" as to what the results of my year's research would be, but now that the material has finally been collated and arranged into what, I hope, will be intelligent and coherent chapters — certain "truths" have become evident.

We are going forward; we are using new materials and technologies; computer chips and software have had a tremendous influence on how we design and what we design — and on how we run retail operations. However, with all of our forward movement into the 21st century and the "Brave New Worlds" still undiscovered — we are holding fast onto the past like a security blanket. It is the umbilical cord that sustains us and nurtures us as we move ahead. As the reader turns the pages of this edition and reads what has been written or quoted from the material provided by the architects/store planners/designers, the reader will find the words "traditional" and "value" reappearing along with other words and terms such as "classic," "old-fashioned," "The '50s," "The '60s," "upscale" and "upbeat." Expect to see "country-style," "casual," "comfortable," "friendly" used to describe markets and gourmet shops as well as cafes, coffee shops and fast food operations and food courts. "Dramatic" and "theatrical" are two more recurring themes that come to the top when reviewing this material. Whether it is a deli — a diner — or a grill with "a foreign accent" — theater and drama are built in with the presentation of the food and the ambience of the restaurant; the lighting and the colors and textures that make the space special and unique. "Different" is always important when there is competition and the designers/architects who

created the shops, stores and spaces you are about to visit all tried to create "different" and "unique" environments that will attract and then bring back the patron. But, the design vernacular they started with — the decorative elements — the cliches that graphically say more than words to create that special ambience — that vernacular is often of the past. You'll know that the produce is "country fresh" because it is displayed atop weathered crates and cartons or overflowing from scarred barrels. In a minimalist, contemporary setting the addition of rattan and wicker baskets and trays and sprays of wheat will suggest a "homey wholesomeness" — a recognition of how things used to be — of mom's cooking and baking — of traditions and values of a bygone time.

The 30-and-under crowd who fill the diners, cafes and coffee houses — who dine on fast foods in and out of food courts — they are the ones who are now reliving the '50s and '60s of "Father Knows Best," "Leave it to Beaver" and "Ozzie and Harriet." Though they may "laugh" at the quaintness of those family lives — the "wholesomeness" of the family unit, they often envy the sense of security that came from the "family values" they are watching caricaturized on the TV screen. The "American Grafitti" of the 1950s is alive and well in the '90s and the old-fashioned diners are still the popular meeting and dining spots for the younger generation. The 50-and-older groups is dining out more and they are also shopping for the gourmet foods and specialties — as are the people in the 30s and 40s. The older group is experimenting with foods but they are concerned with good health, proper nutrition — and, yes, values. To them the signs and symbols of the past mean security. When you are in a safe, sound and "familiar" setting you are more willing to be daring and adventurous. You know where you are — you have something to fall back on.

As in the previous edition, I have tried to group the material into chapters that focus on the various places and ways that the presentation of the food plays a major role in the design of the setting.

Chapter One combines Delis with assorted Take-Out/Eat-

In operations. The premise here is that to see it is to want it — and you don't have to wait till you are home to enjoy it. More and more seating areas are being added to gourmet prepared food shops and delicatessen so that, like in our opening chapter, the Eat-In sometimes overwhelms the Take-Out and the business becomes more of a restaurant than a catering service. The "instant gratification" bit may be left over from the '80s but even the markets are providing seating areas and becoming "food courts."

There are a variety of food specialty stores presented in Chapter Two. They range from the miniature Harrod's food hall in the Heathrow Airport and several other airport and roadside food shops — here and abroad — to the select gift food stores like Hediard in Paris and noted chocolatiers such as Godiva and La Maison du Chocolat. For the nostalgia-ists, there is Roger's century-old establishment in Vancouver and the new/old Copper Kettle Candy & Cone shop in Whittier, CA. There are also wine and spirit emporiums, bake shops and pasta shops and even a bulk food operation that has moved into the mall scene.

The thrust of Chapter Three starts with Coffee and the epidemic of coffee stores that is proliferating across the country and cashing in on the newly discovered popularity and expansion opportunities in gourmet blends of coffee beans. It isn't far from a coffee bean shop to a coffee serving shop and many of the coffee stores are becoming coffee houses where the freshly roasted, ground-to-order beans share the spotlight and space with an assortment of freshly brewed coffees and espressos. The Coffee Shops overlap with the Coffee Bars and what the French call cafes. For this book we consider "cafes" those places where light repasts are served — with coffee. Expanding on "light repasts" we have included Cafeterias with a special group of Employe Cafeterias that are becoming an integral part of corporate headquarter space allocation and design.

Chapter Four is filled with theatrical experiences in dining rendered international by the scope of the foods being offered. We start with the American grill concept which now often has a Southwestern accent — and also the Diners that are part of the American life and dream as captured in movies like "Diner" and "American Grafitti." They are as wholesome, traditional and nostalgic as mom's home cooking, apple pie and freshly ground and prepared hamburgers. From there we highlight the fish houses and then a smattering of foreign tastes including Italian, Asian and Mexican. In almost every case the exhibition/display kitchen plays its part in the unfolding drama in dining — as well as the food which is presented on carts, on bar tops or at the frenetic Sushi counter. Let us not ignore the effect that the aromas wafting out from the wood-burning ovens or the smoking chips on the grill have on the patrons who are also within sight of the finished products.

Chapter Five focuses in on a variety of fast food operations — many in food court locations — but some free-standing. Here too, the emphasis is on ambience and presentation; on food set out under effective and flattering lights to show off color and texture and to stimulate the taste buds as well as the eyes. For the concluding food courts we have highlighted some that we feel are representative of the current trends and looks; the kinds of materials and architectural motifs, the lighting and the landscaping. Some we have selected because we felt that their locations were quite unique and an indication of things to come.

In our final chapter we go back to the very beginning — where it all starts — we head for the markets. Today markets are also "specialized." The re-emergence of the Farmer's Market as a retailing entity is a perfect example of how we are looking backwards as we head into the future. The projects we have selected show some very new examples as well as some quite traditional ones — but it is not difficult to recognize the commonality of the presentation; the emphasis on abundance and freshness.

We hope that you will find this book a satisfying morsel; a delight to the senses as well as a presentation of sensible ways to delight prospective patrons. Enjoy!

Martin M. Pegler, S.V.M.

FOOD

RETAIL DESIGN & DISPLAY 2

EAT-IN / TAKE-OUT DELI'S

AND DELICATESSENS

"Would ye both eat your cake and have your cake?"

John Heywood (1497-1580), Proverbs

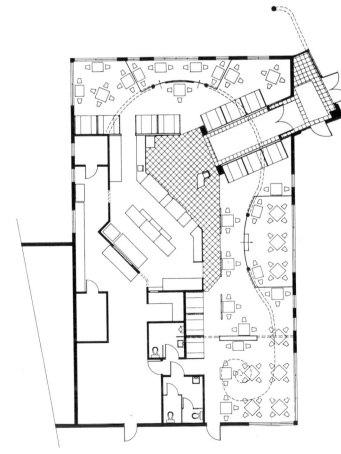

ISAAC'S AT ROSSMOYNE

Mechanicsburg, PA

Isaac's is "more than a deli" that serves "lunch with life"! It is a growing chain of deli/restaurants in the Lancaster area of Pennsylvania and the central theme in each design is the focus on the open kitchen concept. "This provides an atmosphere of high energy, both in service and visual stimuli, and embodies the Isaac's workplace philosophy." With the cooking being visible, there has to be an emphasis on the freshly prepared quality of the food.

The wooden booths are constructed of a wainscoting material known as "Philadelphia fencing" and they are another Isaac's design signature. The very first Isaac's was furnished with similar booths constructed of materials left over on the site. The booths provide intimacy — if not the greatest comfort — but since Isaac's needs a rapid turnover — these straight backed seats are just fine for the "quick" meals served quickly. Also bold design elements like neon and bright colors add to the pace of staff and patrons.

To define smaller dining areas in the 4200 sq. ft. space, platforms with handrails were incorporated into the design. "Each location is incorporated into an area which could be considered semi-private, to draw corporate clients to Isaac's for lunch meetings." The same space is open and accessible to the rest of the restaurant when not being used for the special small groups.

In keeping with the owner's interest in plants and exotic birds, the design elements include built-in aquariums, framed bird prints, trellises and planters and the "exotic" colors that go with the Fiesta Ware service, the menu of sandwiches with bird's names and the hot pink flamingo that has become the logo for Isaac's.

Design: Elvin Hess Designs, Lancaster, PA
Arch: Greenfield Architects, Ltd., Lancaster, PA
Photos: John P. Herr, Lancaster, PA

SHOPSY'S DELI

Yonge St., Toronto, Ontario, Canada

The criteria was to relocate a thriving, well established restaurant/take-out operation that had been successful for over 50 years and still keep "an ambience of a bye-gone era where people of today — of all ages and styles of dress — could feel comfortable at any time of the day or night." It meant "recreating the '50s look as perceived by people of the '90s."

The transformation was achieved by using materials and motifs of the past in an eclectic mix that, together, affect a warm, friendly and "comfortable" background for the food. Natural woods rub up against laminates and naugehydes that suggest the '40s and '50s and shiny aluminum patterned panels and glistening chrome edged cases and tables appear next to white walls and atop white mini-tile floors banded and patterned with contrasting tiles. A variety of "old fashioned" milk glass drop lights add to the nostalgia theme as do the rows of complexion bulbs that highlight the deli counters that are so effectively presented up front.

"History is established through each entrance as they take you down a unique path of history of the establishment and its area. The store has a clean, contemporary image which was attained by the use of materials and fittings. The differing levels were utilized to create a stage effect and along with the lighting accentuate the preparation area as a focal point in the restaurant."

With warmth and charm, the designers have created a "restaurant with a history" for their clients.

Design: Martin Hirschberg Design Group, Toronto, Ont.

BLOOM'S N.Y. DELI

New York, NY

In a sophisticated, mid-town location, the designers came up with this contemporary interpretation of a N.Y. Deli. The term "N.Y. Deli" — to most New Yorkers past the age of 35 conjures up images of green pickles and red peppers stuffed into big, fat mason jars — of white marble (the real thing) topped tables, small, comfortable body-hugging chairs and — if you are over 60 — sawdust scattered over a floor of tiny octagonal-shaped tiles. The pickles and peppers are here; now they are used as a recurring decorative element on shelves and in shadow boxes and as a colorful accent in the neutral environment of white, black and natural wood tones. The floor is re-born in terra cotta ceramic tiles patterned with squares of white and a black and white checkered pattern reappears throughout the store; on the walls behind the glass and brass trimmed deli counter down to the napkins used on the tables.

The lighting is soft and easy — creating a comfortable and relaxing ambience; the raised, up-lit, coved ceiling defines the sitting area from the take-out space. Throughout, the designers have amusingly played with memories of the past to create an interior for today with nostalgic touches like hanging salamis and braided twists of garlic — with ketchup bottles blatantly displayed on each table — old-time scales and artifacts (some "collectibles" and some "kitch") but all together they provide a side-show to the main attraction of the food in the cases.

Design: Dorf Associates, New York, NY

FAME DELI

Columbus City Center Mall, Columbus, OH

Fame Deli's owner wanted "an upbeat contemporary store" that would reflect their eclectic menu (from gyros to chef salads) and make the cafe stand out amongst the mall's line of food vendors. Located in the upscaled Columbus City Center Mall, Fame Deli draws the patrons from the shoppers in the mall and also from the local downtown business people.

The interior contrasts classical lines with an unusual combination of colors to create an inviting interior. Pastel laminates mix it up with the bright, shiny metals in the fun, lighthearted ambience. A variety of patterned laminate table tops provide visual interest as does the metal and light sculpture logo that is repeated on the cups and on the take-out packaging. Classic chrome pendant lights on curved stems and wood on the food bar provide a warming contrast to the "bright bouquet of paint and laminate colors," the ribbed glass and the metal accents that add a high-tech attitude to the overall design.

The central focus in Fame Deli is on the "eating bar." By creating the unusual shape and fabricating the counter out of both high tech and classical materials, the bar becomes yet another arresting feature and draws the customers farther into the store. Twin columns, at the entry, cut into the counter top where they are internally illuminated up to the ceiling.

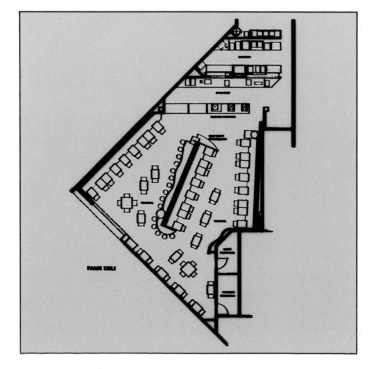

Design: The Chute-Gerdeman Corp., Columbus, OH
Designer: Paul Lechleiter
Graphics & Signage: Elli Chute Gerdeman

SCHWARTZ BROS, DELI

Rainier Square, Seattle, WA

Located on the uppermost level of the elegant and refined, vertical, in-town Rainier Square is a bit of old New York — and a heavy dollop of nostalgia. The Schwartz Bros. Deli is a surprise! · It's not quite what one expects to find in this marble encased mall where gentle piano music rises up from the central court below to the light filled deli above.

One whole section of the food operation is set aside for the traditional and active deli which is bright with light from the peaked glass roof overhead and the pendant milk-glass lamps that illuminate the glass cases on the multi-colored/multi-patterned tile floor. Stand-up tables and some small sit-down ones are provided for people on the go. Recessed under a lower ceiling is a maze of straight-backed booths capped over with a white wood trellis that tends to affect an even more intimate feeling for the dining area. The ceiling is graphically decorated with the Schwartz Bros. name and colorful paintings of Seattle scenes fill in the perimeter walls of the restaurant. The white glass lamps reappear in this area to provide another touch with the past that has already been established by the vinyl upholstery on the booths and the plastic table tops.

Photos: MMP/RVC

Design: Arthur Bloom, owner/operator
Photos: MMP/RVC

RIGATONI

Rockville Centre, NY

When an architect loves a skillet and a chef's toque as much as his drafting tools, it isn't long before he combines his two loves to find contentment and success — and a gourmet food shop/cafe is born. The architect/designer/owner, Arthur Bloom, put all of his passion into recreating the kind of casual — but fine — dining shop he had personally experienced in Italy. Undaunted by the long, narrow 1400 sq. ft. space, but in a prime location for his -venture, he has created a theater for food with seating for 50 patrons who can watch the performance that goes on behind the European style curved glass showcases on the long wall and in the glass enclosed kitchen beyond it. Diners can watch their food being prepared to order or see breads, pastries and "home-made" pastas being made. For those who prefer "to take-out" rather than "eat-in," the glass cases and the counter tops are laden with freshly prepared dishes and salads. Up front, near the entrance, a selection of packaged goods and imported delicacies are presented on metal grid fixtures.

To open up the long, narrow space and to make sure that the "action" can be seen from any seat in the house, the long wall of the dining area is mirrored. The decorative scheme of the store is black and white, a checkerboard pattern, white ceramic tiled walls and atmospheric, but efficient, ceiling fans. The daily specials are hand written, in chalk, on slate-boards mounted between the mirrored panels. To create the proper atmosphere, Juno theatrical-type track lighting is used.

In the short time that this shop/cafe has been open it has already outgrown its space and the demand for "seating" is increasing. When a show is a "hit" — you take it out on the road and Arthur Bloom is taking this one to Woodbury, NY where he will stage another version of Rigatoni.

JOEL'S DELI

Atlanta, GA

Joel's Deli is a renovation of three existing restaurants that were located on the street level of a parking garage. The new design is bright and light and sharp enough to appeal to the students and faculty of the University situated next to the garage. All the spaces are unified into a single homogenous entity by a color scheme of red, white and black with a palette of neutral grays used to fill in between the dominant colors. The strongly patterned black and white checkered floor, laid diagonally, also unifies the spaces with flecked black tiles used to cover the steps that connect the different levels. The same flooring material is employed to border the salad bar-in-the-round and the service counters that line up in the service area.

Curved lines are introduced into the design scheme to add a warm and gracious note; from the bullnose endings of the salad bar to the curved wall that separates the serving area from the seating space. That arced wall, painted a medium gray, carries the curved shelf provided for diners who prefer a stool at a bar to a chair at a table. The same sweeping line appears on the previously mentioned steps. The lighting combines the recessed fluorescent luminaires with incandescent spots over the food service area.

Design: KRA Inc., Atlanta, GA
Photos: James Roof

DAVID'S DELI

The two story, long and narrow building was specially built to house David's Deli — and to fit the site. In a district that is already booming with dining and entertainment establishments, the red neon outlined building with its glass block and stainless steel trim does make a statement. It says "art deco" — and the statement is elaborated upon inside.

The concept is "an art deco diner of the 1940s" and when the project was reviewed in the Canadian Interiors magazine, it was described as "a perfect illustration of total design. It is all of a piece with ceramic tile, stainless steel, glass blocks and neon of the exterior merging flawlessly into the interior applications of these materials." The mint green and black color scheme — with red accents — replays the green facade tiles and the ribbons of red neon that also stripes the store's interior. The neon is recessed in a channel that runs beneath the bulkhead that camouflages the HVAC system. To either side is an open chrome ceiling grid that hides the track lights situated above it.

The chairs are black as are the deep table edges and chrome table supports, moldings and trim sparkle throughout the space. Glass blocks and gentle curves also echo the exterior architecture and the decorative details like the pendant lamps and the wall sconces that are also art deco inspired.

Design: Martin Hirschberg Design Associates, Toronto, Ontario
Design Team: Martin Hirschberg/Robert Lozowy
Architect: Clarke Darling Downey

Pennsylvania Ave., Washington, DC

In keeping with a tradition achieved with many other American Cafes that appear on the East Coast (from Maryland down to Virginia), the emphasis here is on food — beautifully prepared and arranged — to be eaten in or taken out. Many of the "cafes" are located in active malls or retail locations like the view of the one to be found in Washington's Union Station (see right), but this American Cafe Express is located on Pennsylvania Ave. and 17th St. — in downtown Washington, DC.

The black and white tile floor is an American Cafe design signature and the food service area is all white tiles and laminates accented, underscored and enlivened with red and black. Neon signage makes it easier to locate the food of choice and the movement through the check-out counters is fast and easy. A dining or seating area is provided one flight up and between the brilliant red and well illuminated perimeter wall and the multi-colored, textured step-up wall keyholed with blocks of solid color — the way up is not hard to find. Red neon zig-zag lines sizzle on the ceiling — adding excitement and also a sense of direction and destination. Throughout the space the spots, on tracks or on pipe stems, are lowered from the two story high ceiling to get them closer to the objects they are to highlight or enhance.

Design: Smith, Blackburn, Stauffer, Washington, DC

E.A.T.S.

Madison Ave., New York, NY

Set on Madison Ave. amid designer shops and art galleries is E.A.T.S. — an elegant setting for lunch, tea, dinner, or just dessert. If munching and lunching can be fashionable, then this is as fashionable as it gets from the display of dozens of different types of breads and rolls up near the entrance window — to the brilliantly lit array of prepared foods on gleaming metal and white counters and cases — to the dessert station weighted down with pastries, cakes and calories — to the romantically lit, mirror filled European-style cafe area beyond. The large front windows allow the daylight to flood the "take-out" area and the food on view there as well as the sitting area on the opposite side.

The black and white checkered floor runs through the entire space unifying what is actually two adjacent spaces into one flowing entity. An efficient staff of white-smocked attendants stands behind the long glass cases ready to serve. Gleaming coffee cannisters and packaged imported foodstuffs are lined up on the rear wall over the preparation area. Merchandise is displayed on the case tops in straw baskets highlighted by the recessed incandescent lamps in the ceiling.

The cafe area has a continental flavor with small white-topped tables surrounded by light-looking, bentwood chairs painted black. Supporting columns are decoratively painted charcoal gray and fresh cut flowers add colorful accents. However, it is the well lit and amply provided dessert station that is the focal point that draws the diners' eyes in the mirror wrapped interior.

Photos: MMP/RVC

HALE & HEARTY

Lexington Ave., New York, NY

Located on Lexington Ave. — just a few blocks north of Bloomingdales — is this new gourmet food shop that does have a special appeal. Hale and Hearty combines good food with good health and the prepared foods are low in fat, low in sodium and low in cholesterol — and just right for the "health-conscious" uptowners who jog in Central Park. According to the review in New York Magazine, the foods are "delicious and dynamic — unlike most sensible foods."

The designers had to create a "wholesome and healthy" look that would still be compatible with the smart, upscaled ambience these shoppers have come to expect in this area. A life-size, papier mache chef complete with toque, apron and saucepan welcomes the take-out/eat-in patrons up front. He symbolizes what's new in the old art of gourmet cooking. The interior of the 1500 sq. ft. shop is warm and countrified; filled with earthy colors

and provincial textures and touches like the stenciled border on the fascia over the wooden wall cabinets and the flower baskets hung off the wall. Copper metal lamp shades shield the incandescent bulbs that enrich the colors of the prepared foods on view in the glass-faced counters and on the wooden table at the rear of the space. Everywhere natural wicker baskets are used to hold baked goods or for the show and sell of packaged products. Tempting desserts, under glass domes, are presented at eye level to tease and entice the shopper, but since they are "healthy" (no butter, no egg yolks and no cream) — they are not really "sinful."

In her review of this shop, Barbara Costikyan of New York Magazine said, "Hale & Hearty is not a diet or health-food shop, but a place to eat well — be healthy — and have it all." And it's nice to be able to have it all in such a warm and inviting setting.

Design: L. Bogdanow and Associates, Architects, New York, NY

FARMERS MARKET

Atrium Court, Fashion Island, Newport Beach, CA

More than a market — and not quite a food court, but a mixture of both — was recreated in what was formerly the JC Penney department store on the Fashion Island property.

The market has "a casual atmosphere with a sensory appeal of a European marketplace." To achieve the desired effect, the designers used natural, hard-wearing materials and finishes and special furniture like the French bistro chairs. Custom designed maple banquettes and stand-up tables define the edge of the seating area while they also provide alternate dining options.

A relaxed and colorful circulation path makes this marketplace unlike any other food court; it all adds to the open air, free and easy feeling of the space. The paving design includes French limestone, granite and mosaic tiles in fanciful patterns and the concrete floor is textured and colored to simulate the paving usually associated with Italian piazzas.

What also makes this eat-in/take-out center such a visual pleasure are the three-dimensional, often sculptural, storefront designs of the various shops and stalls that feature an eclectic and imaginative mix of materials ranging from Raja slate to brushed stainless steel.

To keep this marketplace looking like a unified design though filled with individual expressions, the RTKL group designed all the interior and exterior signage as well as the directories and the elevator and escalator graphics.

Design: RTKL Architects, Los Angeles, CA
Design Team: Paul F. Jacobs III, principal-in-charge;
*   Jay Clark, A.I.A./Louis Troiani, A.I.A./*
*   Kevin P. Barbee/ Patrick Belyea/Steve Svetlik*
Photos: Toshi Yoshimi

BAKER McSWEENEY'S

Dundes St. E., Mississauga, Ontario, Canada

Baker McSweeney's was originally designed as a take-out bakery/eat-in restaurant — and it was designed with expansion in mind. It is situated in an industrial park, on a major thoroughfare, so not only is it filled at lunch time with workers from the surrounding area, it is also open to the traffic that passes by on the street.

The ambience is casual and relaxed and the color scheme makes it a comfortable and cheerful place to be. Black and white tiles are combined into checkered borders that run along the perimeter walls like wide "chair rails" and they also decorate the white tile faced counters. Light natural wood is seen everywhere in the design; as the deep crown moldings at the ceiling — as wide swathes on the floor — as a decorative casing for the HVAC

system that angles its way across the ceiling — for shelves and molding strips. To achieve a balance between old and new, the designers incorporated a soft blue and candy pink into the color scheme. "The combination of hard textures and 'soft' accessorization and display lends a feeling of wholesomeness and goodness." Note the use of wheat, grains, corn and fruit along with color filled graphics in the presentation of the baked goods and prepared foods up front — and in the cleverly designed HVAC bulkhead above.

Design: Martin Hirschberg Design Group, Toronto, Ontario
Canada

CITY BAKERY

W. 18th St., New York, NY

The 1800 sq. ft. space is located in a 70 year old building on a side street off lower Fifth Ave. which is developing into a fashionable area of shops, boutiques, advertising agencies, photographers' studios and architects' offices. In this up-and-coming area with a sophisticated client in mind for the special baked goods and prepared foods, Wayne Turett and Associates produced this simple, straight-forward and ultra sophisticated solution for a bakery/cafe for people of "taste."

Making full use of a long, narrow space and the 20-foot ceiling height, the area is light; filled with the daylight that comes in through the large glazed expanse up front and the artificially produced "daylight" that comes through the two giant "windows" in the rear. These "windows" are actually fiberglass panels framed in mullions set in the wall that separated the bakery/ kitchen from the rest of the store.

When this store was reviewed in Hotel & Restaurant Design, Mayor Rus described it this way, "The firm's decidedly unfussy design incorporates a variety of recontextualized industrial elements assembled with restraint and playfulness that manage to avoid the tedium of overly self-conscious iconoclasm." The entrance wall is textured with white cake boxes set in a pattern on the white wall. Bolts in the wall serve as both menu holders and coat hooks while a paper roll dispenser, applied to one of the piers, becomes a clever "sign board" that features the specialties of the day.

Almost everything in the architectural and design scheme is white, black or beautiful satin finished stainless steel. Note the cake trays that hold the baked goods up to eye level and the galvanized ducts that extend out from the wall behind the

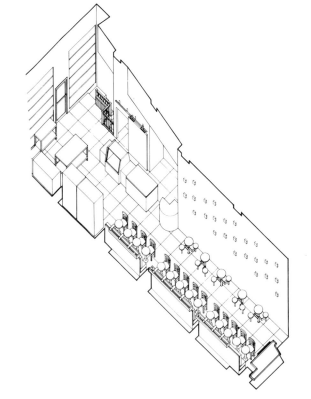

banquettes that serve as magazine holders. Like the bolts, the paper roll, and the cake boxes — these are everyday and industrial materials given a new meaning and expression by the designers to complement the "no frills" confections prepared by the owner/chef, Maury Rubin, and the upscale taste of the clients.

Design: Turett Collaborative Architects, New York, NY
Photos: Paul Warchol Photography, New York, NY

Design: Aumiller Youngquiet, Mt. Prospect, IL
Photos: Steinkamp/Ballogg

BOUDIN BAKERY / CAFE

Schaumburg, IL

Just as a cable car and the Golden Gate Bridge say San Francisco — so does the name Boudin's Sourdough Bread — to anyone who has ever tried it. The notoriety began out in San Francisco and it has been moving eastward ever since. Now the name has been expanded to include the words "and Cafe" because so many people come in to sit down and enjoy the freshly baked rolls and breads, the sandwiches and special platters as there are those who come in to buy the baked goods to go.

This Bakery and Cafe opened recently in the mall in Schaumburg, IL after establishing the name and fame in downtown Chicago and several Chicago locations. The facade suggests an old fashioned bakery with its mullioned display window and the heavily wood paneled and framed basic construction. The inside also says "old fashioned," "homey" and "traditional" and it's all done with the materials — the textures and the colors. It starts with the natural baked tile floors and extends up to the weathered, rose colored brick wall; from the copper valance over the baker's rack display on the wall behind to the white ceramic tiled counter up front. Holding it all together and adding its own toasty warm bit is the muted gold color of the walls surrounding the product display up front and the seating area at the rear.

Over all this visual assault to the senses there is the subtle but stimulating scent of the freshly baked products coming from the wall ovens and filling the air in the shop and sending the aroma out into the mall. Combining the senses of smell with sight leads to taste which always wins out at the Boudin Bakery and Cafe.

HOLLYWOOD DELI

Columbus, OH

Situated in a busy mall, the Hollywood Deli steps out to greet the potential patrons on the aisle. Black and white checkered tile bases zig and zag their way back into the body of the shop carrying glass cases on top with a vivid presentation of fruits and vegetables, of foods to go or to be made into sandwiches or platters to stay.

The same black and white pattern of tile is used to pave the floor inside where white tiles face the counters that are service height. The crisp black and white motif is also carried through on the sign-boards and signage inside the store and even the track system on the ceiling is a combination of the two contrasting colors. The spots are reinforced, in the lighting plan, by recessed incandescent floods that provide the ambient light. Colored graphics and the food presentation starting with the cornucopia of fruits in the cases up front add sparkling, bright colored accents to the black and white color scheme.

Design: The Chute Gerdeman Group, Columbus, OH

"Serenely full, the epicure would say, 'Fate cannot harm me — I have died today.' "

Sydney Smith, 1771-1845

HARROD'S FOOD MALL

Heathrow Airport, England

In our first book on food presentation, Successful Food Merchandising and Display, we featured the famous Harrod's Food Hall in the venerable landmark building located on Brompton Rd. in London. It would have more than an oversight if it hadn't been included since the name Harrod's has become synonymous with fine foods and food presentation.

Today, the visitor who, for one reason or another, commits the unpardonable sin of omission and doesn't get to shop the Food Hall in London, gets a reprieve. He/She has a last chance before boarding the plane at Heathrow Airport to sample and shop in the miniature Food Hall set up in the airport.

The small space, open to two major aisles in its corner location, is basically one long wall and one short one with free standing gondolas and features tables filling up the central space. Rich

mahogany stained woods appear on the floor fixtures and on the wall shelves, counters and cases as well. The wood also is liberally applied as moldings and trim. All that wood plus the black on white tiled floor and the photomurals that reproduce the ornamental tiles and mosaics of the original Food Hall all add a sense of history and tradition to a very "now" space.

Milk glass globes hang down from the ceiling to add light and atmosphere to the shop which is also illuminated by the contained tubular fluorescent strips in the floor and wall fixtures.

Up front, on the main aisle, a series of green canopies (the Harrod's color) carry the Harrod logo and they suggest a class storefront. An octagonal shaped display case, tiered with gift food suggestions, is decorated with the usual Harrod's style and elan extends out into the trafficked aisle.

Design: Harrod's Store Planning and Design Department
Photos: MMP/RVC

GEORGE'S INTERNATIONAL MARKET

Ninth Avenue, New York, NY

George's International Market is as specialized as a store can get. This street front operation is located on the unglamorous, non upscaled Ninth Ave. in New York City — just a street or two from the busy bus terminal on W. 40th St. The area is a "local" market street and the shopkeepers use the pavement in front of their shops to show off the unique and exotic food products they carry. If they still had push-carts in the gutter — this could be New York in the 1920s and '30s. Here fruit and vegetable stores are sandwiched in between butcher shops with carcasses hanging on hooks in the windows — with bakeries stacked with crusty breads and unusual cakes — Italian Specialty stores showing off colorful cans of imported olive oils and George's; a Greek/Turkish/Near Eastern specialty food shop. Together these store overwhelm the pedestrian with sights, smells and colors.

George's, in particular, beckons to the shopper with all of the above. Not only the locals and the "ethnics" shop here, this store has a special appeal as a "Mecca" for gourmet chefs and cooks; for people who enjoy cooking and can find the special spices, herbs, beans, or whatever, to make their dishes authentic. Instead of custom designed "fixtures" and displayers, the staff at George's does it with actual barrels, crates and cartons — often the very stamped and imprinted containers that these imported delicacies and staples traveled in from Greece, Turkey or the Near East. The barrels and crates are neatly arranged in the long, narrow store with its worn wood floor. Overhead, ungracious and often unflattering fluorescent tubes flood the interior with a chilly ambience. BUT — the smells of the spices and the generous and abundant presentation of the staples like beans, peas and rice in myriad colors and shapes more than make up for what is missing in decor. Olives — black and green are piled up in oil or brine in giant vats are dates, figs and other imported dried fruits. Specialty

Design: Store owner
Photos: MMP/RVC

breads and sweet stuffs along with an **unending** variety of Halvah — from all over — are neatly **arranged for** the shopper on the counter — up front — near the entrance.

The knowledgeable and **accommodating** staff is dressed for the part it plays. The "uniform" is **almost as** old as the tradition; over their grey cotton jackets they **wear the** overlong and much too wide crisp white aprons that tie around the back and end up in the front. Of course — the uniform isn't complete without a cap. Everything is out and on show; to be seen and smelled — to be tasted and sampled. In a most artless way, the owner of George's has created an artful and arresting specialty store with a genuine flavor because it is all REAL.

HEDIARD

Velizy 2 Shopping Centre, France

Hediard is a specialist food retailer with several branches in Paris though it is owned by Guiness plc in the United Kingdom. "The objective for the design programme was to take their up-market and to build an international brand — blending tradition with modern." Thus, this example of the new corporate identity was installed in the Velizy 2 Shopping Centre and it includes a complete redesign of the company's packaging range.

The shop is light beige in color and most of the wall space is taken with library-type shelving units that all but reach the ceiling. The uppermost shelf becomes a display area for gift wrapped products and packages. In order to accommodate the range of product and also to add a feeling of warmth and a sense of abundance, the climbing shelves are equipped with a library step ladder that rolls about on a brass rail that extends out from the wall units. This way the service people can reach the merchandise on the higher shelves.

The white tiled floor is divided into larger squares by a grid of contrasting black tiles. The floor fixtures are handsomely crafted, like furniture, of natural wood and detailed with a contemporized linenfold pattern. The corner tables carry an array of gift packages wrapped and tied with red ribbons and set out, for emphasis, on a red fabric pad. The recurring note in this mostly wood interior is the red that appears so prominently in the packaging design; the labels and the wrappings. White glass, cone-shaped, pendant lamps hang down over the main cash/wrap counter while recessed lamps in the ceiling along with the up-lights behind the uppermost shelf add to the overall, ambient light. Crates and cartons that the products arrive in — like the wine display up front — serve as on-the-floor elevations while adding to the "abundant" look of the shop's merchandising.

Design: Fitch RS, London, England

Design: Babcock & Schmis Associates, Bath, OH

BOB EVAN'S FARMS GENERAL STORE

Pennsylvania Turnpike, PA

Located along the well-trafficked Pennsylvania Turnpike as well as in resort areas like King's Island theme park in Ohio and Myrtle Beach, are the Bob Evan's General Stores that in addition to arts and crafts, pottery, new/old artifacts, candles and such, also have a large food specialty area which also includes a bakery. These delightful shops turn "pit stops" into shopping sprees where travelers can fill up with local preserves and food products — with cookies and muffins, breads and even sandwich "fixin's."

The feeling is warm and homey — like a trip to the general store in "The Little House on the Prairie" — a century ago — when a brick wall with an enclosed oven really meant freshly baked breads. The peaked roof is outlined with bulky pieces of knotty pine wood left in its natural, un-finished state. The floors are also laid in wood that looks as though they have felt the feet of generations of travelers.

The pine wall cupboards and dressers and the floor fixtures are combined with yellow/gold, mini-print patterned wallpaper, the bushels and barrels, the hand made quilts and coverlets and the assorted "antiques" that are for sale at the other end of the shop. The artifacts are used to embellish the "old fashioned, country-style" theme and all together they further "the warm, homey, mid-America, down-on-the-farm imagery" that the client requested.

Spotlights and pendant green metal lamp shades provide most of the illumination for this collection of earthy colors and natural materials rich in texture.

THE CONRAN SHOP

Fulham Rd., London, England

On the lower level of the Michelin House, which is an Art Nouveau masterpiece, is the food shop in the Conran Shop. It is here in the attractive though compact food area that selected food products are presented — some specially gift wrapped — and all ready-to-go. The white on white space consists of one long white wall banked floor to ceiling with shelves finished with a white laminate. The uppermost shelf carries a display of the assorted products shown against a rich blue fascia illuminated by a hidden band of cool neon. The merchandise on the selling floor, facing towards the aisles that surround the shop on three sides, is presented on assorted light-looking, high-tech, chromed metal fixtures that are combined with metal grids. A track light system, placed out from the wall, washes the packaged products with light while accentuating the displays up on top. Recessed incandescents provide the general illumination for the merchandise arranged on the floor.

SELFRIDGE'S WINE SHOP

Oxford St., London, England

Located in the heart of London's West End is Selfridge's Department Store and its Wine Shop is actually a store within a store. It is larger than many free-standing operations. The shop is adjacent to the newly renovated Food Hall and "it has a tradition of quality and stocks a wide range of products."

The designers selected natural materials to create an atmosphere reminiscent of the wine cellar in a French chateau. Prominently featured in the design are stone, ironwork and wood. The shop is enclosed by a stone-work wall punctuated by steel and glass windows detailed with an iron "x" bracing and a steel arch marks the entrance-way. A stone, glass and timber staircase leads up to the mezzanine where the more expensive wines and spirits are displayed. This upper shop is laid with a timber floor in contrast to the tiled floor on the main level and the low ceiling does create an "intimate" and "underground" feeling even though the space is elevated. All light fixtures were specially designed and the mezzanine area features chandelier-style lighting booms made from wrought iron hoops.

On the main level, a fluted column — part of the original building — becomes a focal point. It is surrounded by shelves that diminish in diameter as they rise up and the unit is topped with a brushed stainless steel crown; the same material that is used to outline each shelf and the base that rests on the marble terrazzo floor. A gentle segmented arch of the stainless steel floats overhead marking the entrance and wood panels serve as dividing walls. A wide horizontal band of wood delineates the mezzanine shop from the merchandise below which is arranged on shelves in a recessed area.

The lighting from overhead is bright and crisp. Wherever possible the designers made sure that the original Selfridge architectural details like the plasterwork cornices and columns were retained to add their dignity and quality to the atmosphere of the shop.

Design: John Herbert Partnership, London, England

Design: International Design Group, Toronto, Ontario

VINTAGES

Hazelton Lanes, Toronto, Ontario, Canada

The main objectives of the project were "to plan and design a wine retail outlet that in addition to the 'connoisseur of wine,' the shop would also be directed to the average customer and it would create an atmosphere that was 'comfortable and friendly' while providing information about the Vintages products."

Located in the upscale Hazelton Lanes — just off fashionable Bloor St. in Toronto — the shop had to live up to its surroundings; be "tasteful and inviting" — without intimidating the shopper. "A low key cellar concept was chosen with an emphasis on wine tasting and consumer information" and though the location was prime center court, it was impacted by the main escalator which restricted the view of the store front along the lease line. By extending the lease line under the escalator, the designers were able to achieve an "arcade" look in the 10 feet of space and they continued the mall finishes and materials through the "arcade." "The impression created a natural extension from the court to Vintages — giving the feeling of the escalators being in the Vintages space proper."

Natural woods, brick faced arches intersecting in both directions, a low ceiling and the judicious use of incandescent lamps affected the desired "wine cellar" ambience. The actual lights

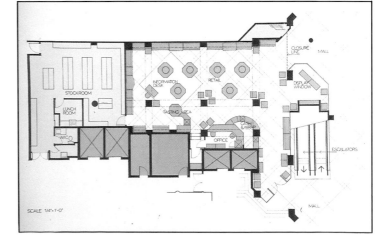

were set above the rustic wood grill that was suspended down from the true ceiling. The centrally located round table joined with the provincial style ladder back chairs make this wine tasting area a focal point in the composition of the shop. The floor is light; it combines tiles of off white, medium gray and terra cotta into a plaid pattern that is occasionally interrupted by brick.

The graphics and signage system is controlled and contained within black metal frames set at right angles to the brick piers. This Vintages is a new concept for the client and it has already been heartily accepted by the customers.

ALLDER'S WINE & LIQUOR SHOP

Duty Free Shop, Vancouver Airport, Vancouver, BC, Canada

The landlord, Transport Canada, was looking for a Canadian theme for this centrally located, 4000 sq. ft. space. They wanted something that would be native and natural to the area.

The International Design Group came up with the "Long House" concept, a structural design that is native to the Indians of the region which includes distinctive characteristics like adzed (or chiseled) beams and columns of mighty pieces of fir wood. The big challenge came in balancing the look of a modern, commercial airport with a contrasting traditional long house structure which is indigenous to the Northwest coast. The central, flat drywall ceiling was changed to a peaked ceiling and a central "fire pit" area was designated as the Wine & Liquor Shop with a grid system drying rack above — both being typical elements found in long houses. These two elements not only added "authenticity" but provided a flexible track lighting system for

the area. In keeping with the "look," the floors and fixtures are made of native woods. Note how the floor is laid in a pattern of concentric circles — "around the fire pit" — which is the concept of this space.

The interior space was designed with wide aisles and a series of inlets or bays with projecting peninsulas used as main feature displays; "creating a semi-boutiquing approach to retailing. The colors and materials inferred from the forest have been chosen to reinforce the concept reflected in the contrasting of natural red, earth-toned woods used primarily for wall fixturing with — when needed — cool green accents."

Energy saving compact fluorescents, halogen par lamps and the skylights "encourage an overall, warm, natural, healthy sunlit feeling while providing full color renditions of products and materials."

Design: International Design Group, Toronto, Ontario

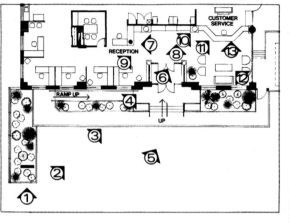

L.C.B.O. SPECIAL BRANDS

Freeland St., Toronto, Ontario, Canada

The L.C.B.O. is the Liquor Control Board of Ontario and this space combines the customer service consignment warehouse with an office area. The problems facing the designers was how to amalgamate the several existing client service areas into a unified, contemporary open concept and make the modern feeling of an office area aesthetically coexist with the "time honored" yellow brick warehouse. They also had to make sure that the design would provide the utmost in efficient customer service to a varied clientele.

The solution included a balance achieved through integrating finishes and details "with varying interpretive perceptions tieing back to either the warehouse or modern office." The strong, bold contemporary lines of the custom designed counters balance the natural marble and bevelled etched glass which is quite sophisticated which is contrasted to the detailing of the metal supports and the magna-grid ceiling. Carpathian elm, low voltage downlights, selected colors, the carpets and the detailing were all chosen to ensure interaction of the two extremes. Thus, "the space was successfully designed to retain the warehouse characteristics while providing an efficient, modern and inviting look with welcome and appeal. The result is a warehouse that melds with today's modern office environment."

Design: Martin Hirschberg Design Group, Toronto, Ontario

Design: Calvin Lau Designs, San Francisco, CA
Interior Design: Visnja Ratkvovic
Graphic Design: Noel Remigio
Photo: Michael C. Lewis

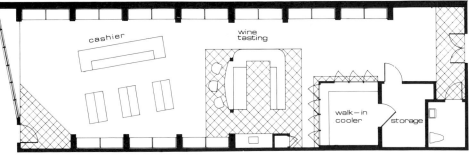

The owners wanted a "comfortable premium wine store with a wine tasting bar as a focal point." With the three owners being astute and experienced wine merchants and also being knowledgeable of the nearby prestigious Pacific Heights neighborhood, the designers were able to turn the whole space into a showroom and display area with no back storage!

To achieve a light, airy and cheerful ambience, the designers used light woods, contemporary style racks, white metal drop lights, soft off-white paint and glass block windows that allow natural light to sift through the store's interior. The decorative color in the shop comes from the liquor bottles and the flamingo mural over the wine bar. It is all that is left of the former wine store

WINE IMPRESSIONS

Laurel Village Centre, San Francisco, CA

that occupied this space and it is interesting to note that the mural indicates where the shop originally ended. From here back was all stockroom. By removing the wall, the store opened up and the supporting columns have been incorporated into the flamingo pink laminate tasting bar that draws the customers to the back of the space.

GODIVA CHOCOLATIER

Pan Am Building, New York, NY

The name Godiva is famous for its top quality chocolates and they are made in the best tradition of the maitres chocolatiers of Belgium. Not only is the merchandise exquisite but the shops that house the beautifully presented and packaged merchandise are also jewel-like — and as taste-full as the products purveyed.

One of the newest of the upscale shops has recently opened in the Pan Am building just off Park Ave. in midtown NYC. As in most Godiva shops, the whole store is on view through almost totally glass facades. Inside all is pretty, pink and plush; from the blushing pink walls to the rosy pink marble terrazzo floor and to the satin ribbons, bows and flowers that decorate the brushed gold boxes. The curved glass counters that stretch completely across the width of the shop are finished with a gold colored metallic laminate base decoratively outlined with frames of black. Black is the accent that appears with gold on the stores signage. The free standing display cubes that appear up near the glass-line to show off the special featured packages are finished in a black laminate and here the cut-out cornered frames are in gold — a reverse of the motif used on the counter bases.

A signature crystal chandelier hangs down in the center of the store adding shimmer and shine to the tiered cove ceiling with its up-light accents. Recessed spots, set into the lowest ceiling just over the counters, provide the warmth that is reflected off the pastel pink walls and the illuminated cases to show the merchandise off at its best.

Visual Merchandising: Mark Nathan Ratcliff
Design: Freil-Bernheim, Philadelphia, PA
Photos: MMP/RVC

LA MAISON DU CHOCOLAT

E. 73rd St., New York, NY

What Godiva Chocolatier is to Belgium, La Maison du Chocolat is to Paris where the first three shops in the operation are located. This shop on tree-lined E. 73rd St. off Madison Ave. is the first American outlet for the French chocolatier. The talent behind the product is Robert Linxe who after 40 years achieved his dream of owning his own specialty gourmet chocolate firm.

The first La Maison du Chocolat opened in 1977 in a former wine cellar on Rue du Faubourg Ste. Honore in the center of Paris' luxury boutique area. The fixturing and design concept for that shop and the ones that have followed was developed by the Bayonne architect, Arnaud Faez. Deep, rich colored wood fixtures are decorated with arrowhead designs — similar to those used to enhance the inverted "V" shaped arches that frame the wall cabinets behind which are constructed of the same wood. Just as the counters are illuminated, so are the wall cabinets with the display of packaged gift boxes and related items. The floor is covered with a splattered marble pattern in gray, black and white. Beyond the display cases and the cash/wrap desk is a glass-enclosed chocolate dipping area where customers can watch the chocolates being crafted. Since the space is long and narrow — and quite dark, the entrance wall (opposite the cases) is lined with mirrors from floor to ceiling.

The recessed lights are incandescent and some light does come through the big display window up front. The store front design looks like a bit of Paris that has been transported to New York.

Architect/Designer: Arnaud Faez, Bayonne, France
Photos: MMP/RVC

ROGERS CHOCOLATES

Government St., Victoria, B.C., Canada

On the busy business street in lovely old Victoria is Rogers Chocolates. What was originally designed in 1903 to house a jewelry store has been adapted to show off the candy products. The space is crammed full of antique charm interpreted in old-fashioned, dark wood wall fixtures and glass-face counters used to present the chocolates. Mr. Rogers, who founded Rogers Chocolates, is a no "johnny-come-lately" on the Victoria scene. He opened his original shop, just across from this one, in 1885 — so this store is a sort of new-fangled one for the firm.

A lovely stained glass hemi-dome floats over the tiled floor entrance into the shop. Marble and copper materials are combined with leaded pebble textured glass to complete the attractive — and attracting facade. Inside the shop, Victoriana is alive and well and thriving. It is furnished in dark woods, marbles and a deep terra cotta color that sort of holds it all together. Together they work to promote the old-fashioned goodness of the Victoria Creams perfected by Mr. Rogers and they are still being hand made from the same secret recipe in the back of the shop. Original and old lighting fixtures and statuesque lamps add to the low-keyed atmosphere of the shop.

COPPER KETTLE CANDY & CONES

E. Whittier Blvd., Whittier, CA

Nearly 100 years ago a pharmacy/confectionery/ice-cream parlor opened for business in the pulp milling town of Davis in West Virginia. The golden oak ornately carved and appliqued wall cases that encircled the store were nearly 11' tall and the cases, made up of 11 sections, covered 90 running feet. In 1985 all this wonderful Victorian woodwork became obsolete as the store was being updated — and everything had to go. The "priceless" woodwork/cabinets went to the avid antique collectors, Bill and Evelyn Thunell. They purchased the "interior" whose ornateness and fine craftsmanship may only be exceeded by the one on display in the Smithsonian Institute in Washington, DC.

For over five years the Thunell's traveled around the country buying additional counters, showcases and accessories of the same period and in 1989 they realized their dream when they opened Copper Kettle Candy and Cones. This store in Whittier, CA has an authentic pressed tin ceiling and old-fashioned ceiling fans with lamps that provide the general light for the re-created store.

The space is filled with artifacts of the turn-of-the-century including several copper kettles that were used for making chocolates back then. There are over 500 kinds of old-fashioned candies available in the glass enclosed cases and in large mason jars on the shelves of the tall oak cabinets or on the white marble-topped counters. Aside from the usual "penny candies," the jelly beans, "jaw-breakers," stick candy, rock candy, and many kinds of chocolate, both regular and sugar-free, there are licorice pipes and pennies, hard and soft "scotties" and even natural licorice.

It is possible to sit in an oak booth or enjoy a malt, a cone or a sundae at the original marble soda fountain with its stained glass and mirror-backed panel. In addition, the Thunells have filled their antique candy store with small gift items amidst the Victoriana that is not for sale.

This imaginative and loving re-creation is part candy store/part museum, and whatever the mix — the mix is working. A second Copper Kettle Candy, Confections and Fancy Foods is scheduled to open at CityWalk near the Universal Studios and the Amphitheater.

Design: Evelyn & Bill Thunell, owners

CHOCOLATE BY MUELLER

Springfield Mall, Springfield, NJ

The long, narrow shop is designed as a series of open-to-the-mall "V" shaped areas connected by an occasional flat window display. Running straight and flat over the long side of the shop and zig-zagging across the shorter side is a burgundy-colored fascia decorated with a scrawling, curvy line on top and a straight ribbon of neon below. The word "Chocolate" makes a dramatic appearance in white neon on the fascia and the rest of the shop name is dimensionally applied to either side of the illuminated word.

The baseboards of the cases that angle in the spaces are finished in a burl wood laminate bordered with burgundy ceramic tiles. The floor combines the warm beige color of the wood with borders of the rich deep reddish purple color. Chromed cube-like cages hang down from the shop ceiling to display, over eye level, a variety of gift package ideas and the case tops are weighted down with candies in big glass jars and other "impulse" items. Focusable spots are attached along the inner edge of the fascia and they light up the cases, the displays in the chromed cubes, and the grid on top.

Design: Office of Charles King, Philadelphia, PA

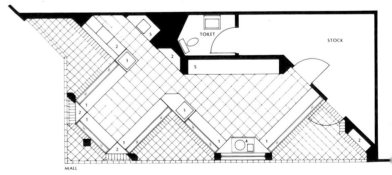

MAUD BORUP CANDY

International Centre, Minneapolis, MN

Like Mr. Rogers of Rogers Chocolates, Maud Borup began making her candies late in the 1800s over in St. Paul. Eventually her market expanded from just her socially elite acquaintances to include the crowned heads of Europe.

For this shop in a mall, the architects created a design that "integrates references to the opulence of the clientele in cold, laced black terrazzo — the all glass display cases with exposed brass connectors and ball feet — the mae wood display tables and cabinets. The gold ball that is surmounted over the angled marble wall behind the cases is an allusion to the Maud Borup international business and the name is prominently displayed on the face of the wall in gold relief lettering. The diamond stone flooring leads the customer from the entry to the cases which are seen on an axis between the black marble wall and the door.

The weighing, packing and wrapping happens on the counters located behind the cases. Hard and pre-packaged candies and card displays surround the front side of the cases — parallel to the storefront. Sinks and storage are situated behind the dramatic angled stone wall that makes such a big impression in the design.

Design: Shea Architects, Minneapolis, MN
Project Manager: Gregory Rothweiler

BOURBON ST. CANDY CO.

Menlo Park Mall, Edison, NJ

Bourbon St. means New Orleans and New Orleans means Mardi Gras; it means color, excitement, fun and frolicking. New Orleans is "The Streetcar Named Desire" and anyone desiring a feast for the eyes and the opportunity to taste the 500 or more bulk selections of candy has only to approach the hollyberry red, hunter green and bright yellow facade. An old-fashioned lamp post with milk glass globes stands to either side of the arched entrance way that carries the shop's name.

Facing the aisle and sitting on the "tracks" in this 700 sq. ft. space is the "trolley car" complete with head light. It is the focal point in the bright and color-filled space as well as the cash/wrap counter. Refrigerated glass cases are housed under the side counters and display a selection of handmade chocolates. Boxed European chocolates and a variety of novel gift items are also displayed on the counter and on the clear acrylic shelving that lines the white walls of the shop.

The display bins are also of clear acrylic and they sit atop a base of storage cabinets of red, banded in green and outlined in yellow. The bins are lined up in three or four tiers and fully on view under the generous lighting provided by the ceiling tracks and the recessed fluorescent luminaires; the candies appear as a fiesta of color and selection.

To add to the New Orleans illusion, the air is filled with a mixture of jazz and cajun/creole music to further enhance the visual presentation. "Re-creating the fun of the corner candy store within an exciting motif was the drive behind the creation of Bourbon St. Candy Co."

Design: Luna Park Designs, Ontario, CA
Bourbon St. Candy: Elizabeth Hughes/Blaine McGrath/ Tom Brown
Photos: MMP/RVC

HOUSE OF ALMONDS

Towne Centre at Cobb, Kennesaw, GA

An oasis where the weary mall traveler can find sustenance that pleases the eye and satisfies the palate is the House of Almonds. The store design and the visual merchandising have become easily recognizable spaces in many malls around the country. The signature fixturing of the walls and the floor fixtures and counters have also become representative of the class product presented with style and good taste.

Warm natural woods are used for the shelves, the bins and counter, and cases that follow around the walls and stand out on the floor. The beauty of the woods and the presentation of the assorted nuts, candies and gift packages are enhanced by the sports that line up on tracks on the ceiling which is painted a deep beige color that blends with the wood tones and the marble tiled floor below. Specially crafted brass bound and studded wooden baskets hold the shelved nuts on slightly raked bases so that the shopper can see the entire assortment presented under acrylic covers. Brass dome lights hang down from the ceiling to light up the products on display. The shelves on the walls simulate a library setting as they extend up to the ceiling. The uppermost area — the closest to the lighting — is recessed into a series of shadow boxes for the display of the handsomely wrapped and ribboned gift packages and baskets.

Since special blends of coffee are now also available in some of the House of Almonds, acrylic-faced bins have been designed to fit inside the modular shelving units that comprise the perimeter of the shop.

Design: James T. Nakaoka Associates, Los Angeles, CA

ZARO'S BREAD BASKET

Danbury, CT

The program was to create a prototype design for an expanding retail bakery chain located in and around NYC. In a typical 2000 sq. ft. space, the shop would have to include in the sales area, display cases for the assortment of baked goods as well as back-up supplies of coffee and soda, etc. They also had to make room for refrigeration and freezer equipment, food preparation areas and on-site baking and dry storage areas. Equally important for the firm but maybe more important for the clientele "was developing design aesthetic that would be acceptable as either an interior shopping mall (shown here), exterior strip center, or even as a free-standing operation.

In the finished design the product gets the greatest visibility in the up front display cases with the high output lighting — or on the shelves behind the serving area which are highlighted with low voltage accent lighting. Black and white tiles are checkerboarded on the base of the angled display cases/counters as well as on the floor in front of them. Old-fashioned design elements like pressed tin ceiling material and pendant ribbed crystal "gas lights" are combined along with natural wood trim and moldings.

The company name is highlighted by neon behind the opaque, pin-mounted brass letters. The fascia that the letters are applied to is also finished with the painted pressed tin. All materials were selected for their durability, ease of maintenance, and immaculate appearance — as well as their suggesting an old-fashioned, wholesome and homey taste experience.

Design: Berger Rait Design Associates, NY

STELLA'S BAKERY

Rockville Pike, Rockville, MD

What can you do when your budget is small and your space is even more limited? Use lots of white — and lots of imagination. This bakery/cafe is situated off the main Rockville Pike and it is a genuine labor of love. Stella Crawley, the owner, at an auction of props and fixtures of a closing downtown Washington, DC department store bid on and became the proud owner of the wood framed arched panels that contain period etched glass artwork. With that at the start, the architects created the niches within which the frames float and that created an architectural expression that changed the small space from an uninspired cube into a special space enriched with planes and softening curves.

The glass and brass curved display cases for the baked products are set atop reclaimed counters that were freshly veneered with white laminate and accented with chocolate brown — the same color that is used on the arch frames and the padded seats that accompany the several small cafe tables in the limited area.

A wide expanse of glass puts the well-lit store on view and the daylight with the recessed incandescents and the white walls and fixtures add up to a delightful, airy ambience in which to shop for cakes or to stop for coffee and something. The lovely marble terrazzo floor is a happy medium between the white and the chocolate brown trim.

Architect: Burgos and Associates
Design Concept: Stella Crawley, owner
Photos: MMP/RVC

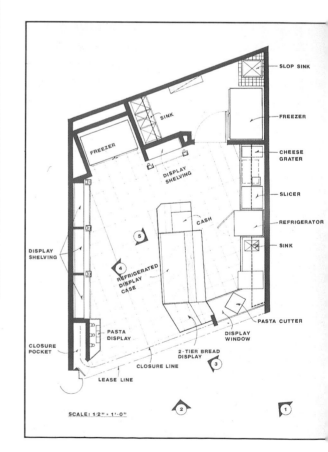

SLOP SINK

FREEZER

CHEESE GRATER

SLICER

REFRIGERATOR

SINK

SINK

DISPLAY SHELVING

FREEZER

DISPLAY SHELVING

CASH

REFRIGERATED DISPLAY CASE

PASTA CUTTER

DISPLAY WINDOW

PASTA DISPLAY

CLOSURE POCKET

CLOSURE LINE

2-TIER BREAD DISPLAY

LEASE LINE

SCALE: 1/2" = 1'-0"

PATISSIMA

Westmont Mall, London, Ontario, Canada

The architect/designers were called upon to develop "an intriguing marketable and graphic environment with mass appeal for the successful retailing of pasta and supplementary products." The ambience and presentation had to appeal to the sophisticated middle to upper class customer.

Using a color scheme of black and white and lots of sculptural and graphic elements, the designers proceeded within the limited space of 375 sq. ft. allotted to the project in the mall location. Up front, above the stepped base covered with the same terrazzo tiles that are used on the floor of the shop the designers put a counter top model pasta cutter who demonstrates, educates and attracts the mall stroller — bringing him/her closer to see what is behind. Inside, the interest is strengthened by custom designed, back lit pasta display boards which graphically illustrate the myriad varieties of pasta cuts available. The possibilities are underscored by the balance of two-dimensional, black and white sculptural

out of "noodle impressions" mounted as vertical exclamation points between the wall mounted shelves. These pieces are also back-lit for further emphasis.

The splattered gray and white terrazzo resilient tile flooring complements the black, white and stainless steel scheme of the area. The rear wall that includes the shiny framed oven is finished in a grid of small black tiles set in a pronounced white grout and the store name panel is prominently placed over the black signboard with white lettering.

Black ceiling tracks equipped with black lamp shades make a square on the dropped, white ceiling and they provide the brightness inside the shop. The spatter pattern and matte black wood store front is enhanced with the illuminated sign over the opening. In the stores that have followed and where a large space was available, seating has been added for some limited food service.

Design: Martin Hirschberg Design Group, Toronto, Ontario

When Mr. Bulky's Treats & Gifts decided to initiate an aggressive expansion program into major malls, part of their strategy was to define the product mix and present their image as an exciting, fun-to-shop environment. That is where the architecture/design firm of Jon Greenberg Associates came in.

To offer the maximum flexibility for the operation, slatwall was used throughout the space. It is wrapped around the dividing walls and it is used up and down, back and forth around the wall graphics and the bulk food bins. The color scheme is a relatively cool one; most of the space is white with periwinkle and blue — accented with black to affect a rather natural but still distinctive background for "the colorful and chaotic merchandise presentation."

The graphics play an important part in establishing the look of the space. Oversized photos fill in some of the wall niches while "clouds" float along behind the cash desk.

The ceiling takes on a "whimsical, layered look beginning at the front with crisscrossing black fluorescent tube fixtures." Suspended down are light boxes that serve as the category signs with lettering on one face and appropriate food graphics on the other. Towards the rear of the space the ceiling "opens up into a blue void" with a white ceiling grid floating beneath it. "The shift in atmosphere is effective and gives the small space a more open feeling." Throughout the store white ceramic tile was used because it looks clean — and is easy to keep clean.

Design: Jon Greenberg Associates, Southfield, IL

COFFEE SHOPS, COFFEE HOUSES, CAFES AND CAFETERIAS

"It is part of a wise man to feed himself with moderate pleasant food and drink — and to take pleasure with perfumes, with the beauty of growing plants, dress, music sports and theatre — and other places of this kind which man may use without any hurt to his fellows.

Benedict Spinoza, "Ethics" 1632-1677

CAFE BRAUER

Lincoln Park Zoo, Chicago, IL

Cafe Brauer was originally conceived and created almost 80 years ago by the architectural firm of Perkins and Hamilton. For the principal architect, Dwight Perkins, it was his finest achievement in Prairie School Design.

Meisel Associates was assigned the task of restoring the landmark building and the food service area located in it. The restoration included duplicating the green tile roof, the Great Hall skylight, and reproducing old fixtures anew as well as other designs and decorative elements of that period.

The main food service area is now a ground floor cafeteria. The charm and refinement of the Prairie School of Design has been re-interpreted by Meisel Associates with the green and white tiled dado below the creamy beige walls; the oak moldings and square colonettes with their simple molding trim; the reproduced pendant fixtures and the white globe lights and brass and wood fans turning around on the green tiled ceiling. The mini-tile floor of white is accented with border designs and "x's" of green tiles laid in a set pattern. The light looking tables and chairs are also finished in a deep teal/green with natural wood trim. A green counter top follows the line of the bay window and patrons, on tall seats, can enjoy the view of the lake and the park while lunching or just sipping.

Design: Meisel Associates Ltd., Chicago, IL

CASABLANCA COFFEES

Chicago Place Mall, Chicago, IL

Casablanca Coffees makes a big impression at first sight in the plush and marble coated Chicago Place Mall, and the impression becomes lasting once the shopper steps into the 670 sq. ft. space. The designers, inspired by the old Warner Bros. classic black and white movie, "Casablanca," — now celebrating its 50th anniversary — created this sharp, stylish and contemporary shop filled with updated Moroccan motifs. The store is small — only 15' wide — and not that much deeper, but the gray, white and flattering peach toned interior does tend to open up the space. The facade which is almost entirely glass has a peaked arch over the double door entry that introduces the inverted "V" motif that adds to the perception of depth — and the illusion of greater height to the store's interior. It also recalls the striped desert tents one fantasizes as being Moroccan. Peach columns, patterned with black and white stripes, flank the opening along with contemporary pedestals that support an assortment of cups and saucers and an introduction to the handsome product packaging available within.

The striped bands of gray and white of the peaked ceiling become a design element on the fascia where it meets the built-in cabinets on the two longer walls of the space. The diagonally laid black and white tiles checkerboard the floor and also seem to expand the width of the shop. Suntanned peach laminates cover the built-in units and combined with the gray and white, and with the black accents, they become the effective scheme for the packaging and gift wrapping of the product which carries the stripes of the ceiling and fascia.

The counter is filled with acrylic-faced bins that reveal a variety of gourmet beans and the shelves beyond carry the cups, carafes, and coffee makers, as well as gift ideas.

Design: Schafer Associates, Oakbrook Terrace, IL
Photos: Briskey Photography, Chicago, IL

LE CAFE ESPRESS

River Falls Mall, Clarksville, IN

Taking his cue from the coffee shops of Europe, the designer evolved this open looking and spacious design for the 400 sq. ft. site in the River Falls Mall.

A pair of square mahogany columns flank either side of the double doored entry which is capped with a wood pediment. The store's name is expressed in brass letters applied to the glass panel that fills in the opening. A whiplash line of neon adds a dash of excitement to the signage and the entrance. Straight ahead, the shopper sees the main stock and display counter with the many varieties of blended coffee beans on view. 48 separate mahogany framed windows are set in groups atop the teal laminate base which is accented with horizontal bands of mahogany. The angled corner cut-outs become display services for the presentation of gift ideas and "go-with" merchandise.

Lining the store are tall mahogany veneered cabinets that also show off a multitude of coffee related products and the shelves are capped on top with a deep mahogany bulkhead that conceals the fluorescent strips that illuminate the merchandise on the glass shelves below. The cabinets that make up the base are used for back-up storage of the products on view above.

At the other end of the coffee-showcase counter, that also incorporates grinders, brewers, scales, cash/wrap surfaces and even a sink and refrigerator under the counter, there is a coffee bar. Here the shopper can stop to enjoy a cup of coffee — an espresso — or snack on some of the delicacies presented in straw baskets on the counter. The pink neon swirl and the store name reappears on the tall rear wall of the shop restating what was evident at the entrance. Brass accents gleam under the spots attached to the metal grid ceilings to either side of the centrally raised portion which is washed by concealed fluorescent strips.

Design: Tony Peddicord, Blue Grass Woodworking of KY, Inc.
Lexington, KY

DALLIS BROS. COFFEE

Ozone Park, NY

It all began with a horse drawn wagon, in Russia, where Abe and Morris Dallis sold their freshly roasted coffees house to house. They migrated to the U.S. and for almost 80 years Dallis Bros. Coffees has been an institution in NY as a family-owned coffee importer, roaster and wholesale distributor. Now it joins the ranks as a retailer in the new shop located in the beautifully restored Victorian style building that also house the Dallis Bros. factory.

With their 650 sq. ft. gourmet coffee outlet, Martha Bear Dallis says, "We are trying to lead an emerging trend of in-store retail roasting that is now on the West Coast but coming up on the East Coast." This store, located next to a Dunkin Donut operation, is catering to quite another clientele with its coffee, tea, desserts, and gift baskets — and with its high pedestaled tables for easy service. The target is "the whole neighborhood of homes and factories — as well as our existing commercial accounts."

The turn-of-the-century decor is warm, friendly and comfortable with lots of golden oak floor fixtures and wall cabinets. The "old" tin metal ceiling is coffered and inset with incandescent lamps, and the floor is an "old-fashioned pattern in assorted color tiles. Decorative tile squares are applied to the bases of the counters that stretch across the wide end of the shop and these counters support assorted packaged goods as well as a glass enclosed case loaded with pastries that complement the coffee or cappuccino that is available. The slate board sign not only provides information

about the specials of the day — it also adds a touch of nostalgia as does the coffee roasting paraphernalia that fills the small, intimate and homey shop.

The building itself has been the recipient of many local awards including 1st prize from the Queens Chamber of Commerce for its "excellence of design." A highlight of the project that recalls the Victorian era is the restoration of the cantilevered roof turret over the corner entrance into the shop.

Design Concept: Martha Bear Dallis
Architect: Marino, Amari Design Associates, Long Island, NY
Photos: Kristine Frampton

SEATTLE'S BEST COFFEE (S.B.C.)

Historic Pike Place Mkt. and Downtown, Seattle, WA

The Pike Pl. Market location was the first of the several retail outlets created by Olson/Sundberg Architects for Seattle's Best Coffee. "The client desired a highly visible design for a retail coffee store selling beans, brewed coffee, espresso and coffee brewing implements."

In keeping with its surroundings, the 1450 sq. ft. space has exposed connections, concrete floors, and it is dressed and trimmed with galvanized sheet metal, steel, ceramic tiles and accents of neon. In addition to the high tech materials used, "Red is used consciously to stimulate and excite the visual senses as coffee stimulates the physical senses." The red tiled barfront and the sizzling ribbons of red neon that frame the curved area behind the bar which has the coffee display bins built into it are the focal points of the design. Besides the all important coffee bean storage and display, the upper area of that arced wall carries educational information. Integrated into the total design is an antique coffee grinder and displays of brewers, grinders and cups.

The second store's design, in Downtown Seattle, highlights "the contrast between the agrarian culture in which coffee is cultivated and the high-tech culture of the United States where the bulk of gourmet coffee is consumed." To this end the designers juxtaposed a high-tech service area against raw-looking walls.

This space is smaller than the first site — only 525 sq. ft. and the designers took advantage of the location in the high fashion shopping district of Seattle to "borrow space from the sidewalk under an elliptical ceiling grid extended above." In affect, the store opens to the outside and tables and chairs, under the open grid canopy, have the relaxed ambience of a Parisian sidewalk cafe. The materials featured in this design include — in addition to the use of the signature red color and the neon — stainless steel and a unique textural "faux" painted wall that combines paint with plaster which contrasts with the high-tech equipment in front of it.

More S.B.C. shops are opening up in Seattle in response to the successful housing and graphic presentation of the products from the bright red bars and signage to the take-out cups and coffee-by-the-pound packaging — all created by the Olson/Sundberg group.

Design: Olson/Sundberg Arch., Seattle, WA
Faux Wall Painting: Eclectic Surfaces
Photos: Robt. Pisano, Seattle, WA

THE FAST LANE SELF SERVICE DRIP COFFEE

SELF SERVICE COFFEE DEPARTMENT

BEANS CO.

Madison Park, Seattle WA

One of the winners in a recent design contest sponsored by the Pacific Northwest Chapter of the Institute of Business Designers was the Beans Co. Coffee Store/Cafe designed by Buffalo Designs. It is entering into the Coffee Shop scene that is an integral part of life in Seattle. Like the word "espresso," the designers tried to capture the essence of that word, both the meaning and the product, and conceptualize it in the 630 sq. ft. space which is only 13' wide! The goal: "Quick and efficient use of space with a clear and succinct product display." Efficiency was priority #1 since the designers had to fit two service lines for the customers' convenience as well as have a compact back room facility in that limited space.

"Symmetry provides clarity." To set itself apart from the other coffee shops/ cafes proliferating in the Seattle area, the designers aimed for a decidedly American look. Rich cherry woods are used throughout since they suggest early American furnishings and copper accents provide the highlights in the case goods. Slate inserts are incorporated into the ceramic tile floor.

Product display and "environmental graphics" give the customers an opportunity to look over the merchandise being offered and to also "realize the owner's commitment to environmental consciousness." Tracks of spotlights follow the long walls of the space highlighting the display of products in the wall cabinets. The service bar that extends across the width of the site tends to visually stretch the opening. Hanging white metal lamp shades light up the counter top and draw the customers to this far end of the shop. Another track light, this one dropping down from the ceiling, illuminates the menu board on the rear wall and the cups and such displayed on the shelves to either side of it. A platform, behind the service counter, gives the server a more commanding view of what is going on up front and helps keep things moving.

Two more Beans Co. shops are on the boards and will be opening soon. They are based on the prototypical design.

Design: Buffalo Design, Seattle, WA
Photos: Chris Eden, Eden Art, Seattle, WA

SPINELLI COFFEE

Polk St., San Francisco, CA

"A lot with a little" is how the Spinelli Coffee Co. describes its 275 sq. ft. Polk St. shop. The glass window wall that opens out on to the street and the generous use of mirrors together create the illusion of a light, open space. However, to complement and enhance the rich, chocolate brown color of the coffee beans, the cabinets and fixtures that furnish the space are deep, dark stained woods "creating an atmosphere of warmth and reveal a fine appreciation for quality."

Lining the walls are brass and glass faced coffee bean dispensers, copper roasters and shelves laden with various coffee brewing and making paraphernalia such as grinders and coffee makers. The counter top is a maze of large glass jars, domed cake stands and myriad straw and wicker baskets, napkin lined, and heaped with tempting Italian biscotti, pastries and specialty gourmet items to go. Christopher Calkins and Arnold Spinelli, who own this shop and designed it along with five other retail outlets in San Francisco, started in the coffee supply business over 10 years ago. They also operate their own roasting plant and warehouse so they offer their gourmet coffees wholesale and nationally through mail order. Like their other outlets, this shop features a stand up coffee bar for freshly brewed coffee.

They make sure that their shops are "a neighborhood fit." They stay as far as they can from the chain store marketing principles — and so far it has worked. Each Spinelli location that opens "has a particular feeling — not unlike a favorite old shoe — of having been around — worn in and comfortable in all the right places." This recent Spinelli shop is "a neighborhood fit" on Polk St. and it couldn't be warmer and friendlier than it is.

*Design: Christopher Calkins/Arnold Spinelli/Robert Quillen/
David Hruska*
Photos: John Bagley

THE COFFEE EXCHANGE

Charlottesville, VA

Located on a walking street in the old commercial part of Charlottesville where city pride and smart shopkeepers are rebuilding the whole area of old and worn buildings — many from before the turn-of-the-century — into a place of boutiques, gourmet food shops and restaurants and arts and crafts outlets is The Coffee Exchange.

This Coffee Shop/Cafe, in a venerable old building, provides the shopper with either an assortment of freshly roasted and ground coffee or the opportunity to enjoy a cup of coffee or a snack at one of the peach cloth covered tables provided with black bentwood chairs. The 2300 sq. ft. space serves both functions and the pungent aroma of freshly roasting coffee emanating from the roaster in the entrance display reassures the shopper — and tempts her.

The interior is divided into several spaces to either side of a central aisle or axis which is accentuated by the peach and terra cotta colored columns to either side that support the longitudinal arcade of arches. In the front space and along one side is the seating area and service counters take up most of the left hand side of the store. The seating clusters are punctuated by glass cases which serve as show-and-sell dividers. They are filled with freshly baked goods.

"The transverse arches and overhead trellis of beams subtly interrupt the narrow, linear quality of the space while enhancing the sense of intimacy of the seating groups." The materials and the color palette of peach, terra cotta, chocolate brown and medium gray "reinforce a sense of continuity."

Design: Daggett & Grigg Architects, Charlottesville, VA
Photos: Philip Beaurline Photography, Charlottesville, VA

THE COFFEE TREE

Forest Hill Village, Toronto, Ontario, Canada

Just as the coffee shop/cafe craze is sweeping across the U.S., it is happening in Canada also. To walk down Robeson St. in Vancouver is to stroll down a street in Paris or Rome with coffee houses and cafes spewing their tables and chairs out onto the street — on the sidewalk — where "people watching" becomes the name of the game. Some of these coffee brew-eries are actually branches of chains established in Seattle — gone north.

In an affluent suburb of Toronto is the new Coffee Tree which combines a freshly roasted coffee retail operation with a small cafe. The designers attempted to capture a European feeling — something sophisticated and a bit Milan-ese for their design concept. The almost all glass facade is accentuated by a double neon check mark over the doorway and by the neon, back-lit, raised signage.

The interior is all white with sharp black accents and lots of stainless steel gleaming in the well lit space. The coffee bean dispensers in their staggered arrangement almost suggest a piece of modern sculpture made up of steel and glass cannisters. The white tiled floor is haphazardly patterned with an informal arrangement of black, aqua, lavender and violet tiles — the same cool, fresh colors that float across the white walls and are arranged in an abstract painting in the rear of the shop. The same colors were selected for the neon accents on the front of the building.

The service counter/bar angles its way from the entrance across the space under a black laminate canopy that frames the roasting activity. A track light system follows the outline of the canopy and illuminates the counter top. The coffee bean roaster that forms an integral part of the operation is featured within view of the expanse of windows.

Several new Coffee Tree shops are already in the work for franchisers.

Design: Martin Hirschberg Design Group, Toronto, Ontario

THE COFFEE PLANTATION

Mill Ave., Tempe, AZ

To make this coffee house/restaurant really stand out from its
surroundings and competition, the designers went back in time
for the concept which they hoped would evoke an environment
reminiscent of where the coffee starts out from. To create the
proper Coffee Plantation ambience, they resorted to a series of

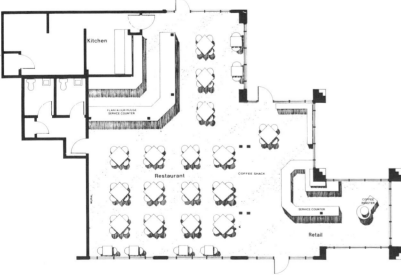

sawn wood fixtures. The main retail presentation is in the Coffee Shack which is dominated by a gleaming copper roaster which is visible from the street — and with the clever venting of the aroma out into the street — it does stop the strollers. For texture and color — "color" as in "local color," the designers added panels of acid washed corrugated metal to simulate the outside of the plantation sheds; burlap bags stamped with countries of origin; painted concrete floors; "palm trees" in big buckets and a custom mural of fields of coffee plants that makes an open air statement in the rear of the space.

The Plantation House stands in the middle of the store and is the focal point of the design. The "two story" structure with its overhanging roof encloses the service area of the restaurant. Framed slate boards hang under the open mezzanine explaining what is available. Built into the "structure" is a glass faced, illuminated counter for those who would rather see the selections for themselves — than read about them.

Dropped metal shades shield the incandescent floods that light up the space and they leave the painted-out ceiling in darkness. It is this that makes it possible to "compress" the Plantation House into a space that isn't actually very high.

cliches which — as combined and presented here — offer a totally new and exciting environment for the retailing of coffee beans — and the enjoyment of coffee with a light repast.

The emphasis is on the gourmet coffee and the complementary products displayed in colorful crates and on custom made, rough-

Design: Habitat, Inc., Tempe, AZ

CAFE NEO

Studio City, CA

"This urban coffee house was intentionally created as a small and intimate gathering place of the '90s — a sort of replacement of the neighborhood bar. The rather close proximity of the interior space along with the abundant visual stimuli encourages patrons to interact with one another."

The space is limited to only 504 sq. ft. and the low budget dictated the use of inexpensive, readily available, industrial type materials. The design followed the materials and part of the budget was used where it would make the most visual impact as on the permanent painted walls and the unique and decorative wall sconces created by local artists and craftspeople.

"The design is a union of strict architectural rules and free form sculpture" using basic shapes and materials. However, the "common" materials were used in uncommon ways to create a juxtaposition.

The stools and chairs were designed in conjunction with an industrial designer and they were produced very inexpensively.

The concrete floor "goes" with the natural, industrial type plywood paneling that is used throughout and the shop is accented with a vivid bluc-violet color and terra cotta colored accessories. A collection of Fiesta Ware pitchers is displayed on the shelves. Track lights follow the line of the counter/bar and send the warm light onto the honey beige surfaces below.

Photos: Ron Pollard

CAFE METRO

S. 7th St., Minneapolis, MN

The Cafe Metro is a bright, contemporary cafe of 1140 sq. ft. that daily has fresh baked muffins and breads to go with the coffee and espresso served here. In addition, a light menu of salads, entrees and ice-cream drinks are available. The space radiates out from the kitchen which is behind the angled colored wall and goes through the baker's area and espresso bar to the service line and the seating beyond.

The service line is made of glass, back-lit, white plexiglass and stainless steel. It sits on a black and white terrazzo floor and curb, outlined and criss-crossed with black divider strips. For seating, banquettes are provided on the walls and at the entries. Stools are located beneath the black laminate shelf that is canti-levered off the salmon colored wall. It can be seen behind the white column that not only becomes the condiment stand — supporting triangular shaped utensil holders — but, like the walls over the

banquette and the aforementioned counter, it is trimmed with framed mirrors. The large blackboard — near the lobby entrance — is angled into the space and acts as the menu board.

The lights over the seating area are "Frisbees" supplemented by the up-light sconces on the wall over the mirrors. Low voltage lamps are recessed in an angular PVC pipe that runs over the service line. In the Baker/Espresso Bar area of the space, the low voltage lamps are set into the sloped gypsum board ceiling. The "frisbee" motif is repeated on the back-lit, plexiglass "Espresso Clock" that is located on the angled wall of ribbed glass seen illustrated above.

Design: Shea Architects, Minneapolis, MN
Project Manager: Gregory Rothweiler

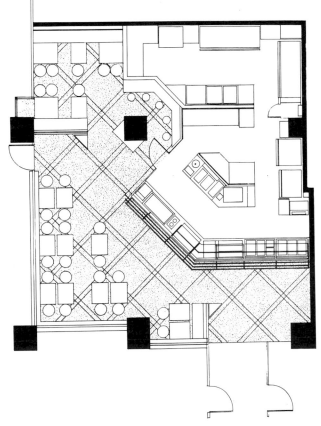

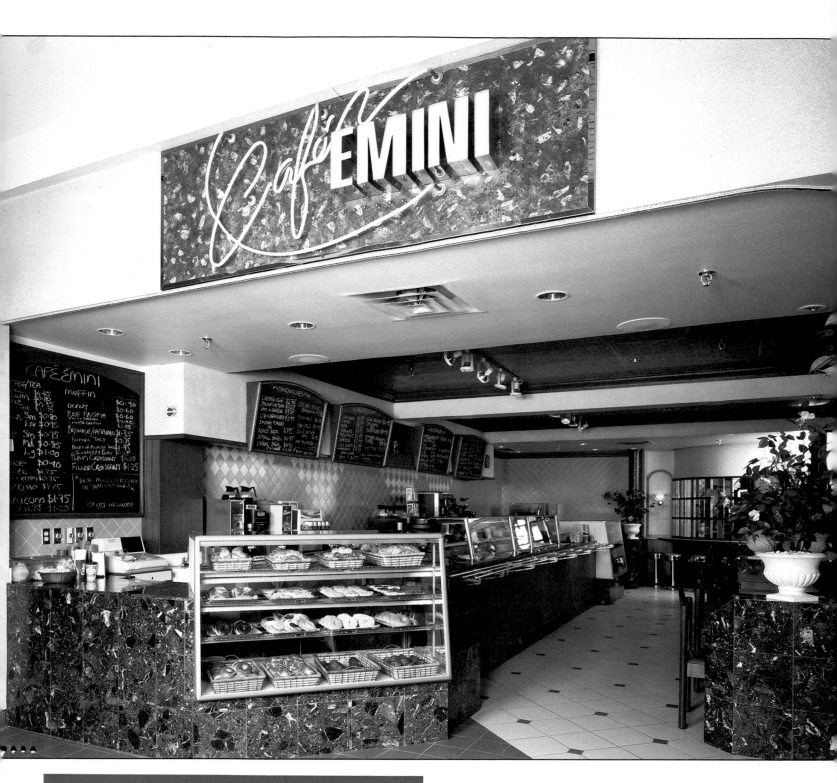

CAFE EMINI

Thornhill, Ontario, Canada

The small Cafe Emini is located on a fashion floor of a mall in Thornhill. Not part of a food court — but rather an intimate space designed to provide a rest and refresh stop in the midst of a full shopping schedule.

The display case of tempting cakes, breads and muffins is cater-cornered off the mall aisle and it is set on a counter faced with tiles of crushed marble chips of dark gray and black. A decorative matching marble angled partition, on the opposite side of the entrance-way offers the shoppers at the tables behind it a degree of privacy but also a view of the passing parade. A faux marble finish serves as a background for the neon and three dimensional, self-illuminated letters above. The same artwork is applied to the columns within the shop. The pattern of the floor, white set with black diamonds, is also angled to receive the shoppers from the mall.

Inside, the area features gray and white tile surfaces on some of the walls especially those behind the long service and display counter. Like the arched frame sign holders and the chairs, the counters are faced with a deep, reddish-brown wood. Mirrors are set into a gridwork of the same wood and they sparkle and reflect the light as they follow the curve of the cantilevered shelf in the rear of the space. Curves and bends and upholstery soften the look of the black and white space which is illuminated with recessed and focusable spots.

Design: Martin Hirschberg Design Group, Toronto, Ontario

DESSERVE SAMPLER CAFE

Mt. Prospect, IL

Like the cafe on the opposite page, Desserve Sampler Cafe is also a mall operation — also done in a palette of black and white but here it is brilliantly accented with touches of bright red. The seating area, on the left, is delineated from the showcases and service counters on the right by the effective change in ceiling heights and color. Uplight wall sconces on the walls in the seating area are complemented by the drop lights and the recessed lighting in the coved ceiling over the food display. The bold, European style black lacquered and curved glass cases are balanced by the black banquettes that line up along the opposite perimeter wall. The white tile floor is enhanced with a fanciful arrangement of black squares and the light looking chairs are upholstered in the red accent color.

Design: Aumiller/Youngquist P.C. Architects, Mt. Prospect, IL
Photo: Judy Slagle

STREET FARM CAFE

O'Hare Airport, Chicago, IL

"Carsons International's goal was to provide a more sophisticated customized menu here than at most airport food concessions." The design, prepared by Green Hiltscher Shapiro Ltd. reflects this. The cafe is divided into several distinct areas; the delicatessen and bakery departments are separated by a large, custom, reach-in beer cooler and a third element is the free-standing liquor bar. "The separate natures emphasize customers' choices; each area is identified with its own individual, neon sign and handwritten menu."

The front of the service area is lined up with glass cases that add to the illusion of a "traditional, made-to-order, food merchant" since instead of pre-made items, there is a display of the uncut makings of the sandwiches along with salads. Spotlights highlight the food offerings.

Commercial kitchen materials are utilized throughout; white work surfaces and ceramic tiles, chrome adjustable shelves and brushed stainless steel. Patterned stainless steel panels, striated tiles, an open grid ceiling, and a checkerboard terrazzo floor provide "visual texture."

Simple contemporary seating is provided for the diners and the space blends successfully with its location in the award winning O'Hare Airport. To the traveler on the run it "creates a perception reminiscent of personalized service and foodstuffs rather than assembly line fast food in design concept."

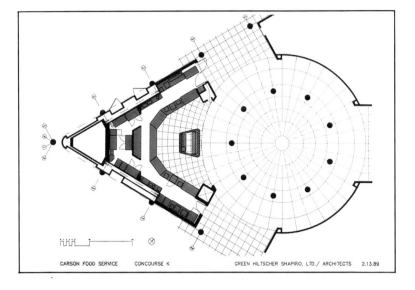

CARSON FOOD SERVICE   CONCOURSE K   GREEN HILTSCHER SHAPIRO, LTD./ ARCHITECTS   2.13.89

Design: Green Hiltscher Shapiro Ltd., Chicago, IL

MARKET ST. CAFE

Market St., Philadelphia, PA

The Market St. Cafe is a 2500 sq. ft. space located on a busy main street in downtown Philadelphia. Though the space is designed with seating at tables and counters for 125 persons, it is expected to turn over 500 seats at breakfast and lunch with many of the patrons coming from offices in the commercial building in which it is located as well as from traffic on the street.

Working with a color scheme that includes natural cherry wood, brass trims, corrugated panels of translucent glass, white tiles and accents of beige, mauve and mulberry, the designers made the space seem open and alive. This was accomplished with the low voltage, high intensity lamps set in tracks on the ceiling that help bring out the colors of the foods on stark white counters.

With the need to avoid long lines usually associated with cafeterias, Dorf Associates provided a "department store" approach to shopping the floor. Overhead, a back-lit, translucent sign panel sawtooths its way over the wood faced serving counters set out on the patterned tile floor. The various selections and options are clearly noted above, above eye-level, and the patron knows which counter to "shop." For the patron's convenience — and speed — the individual pasta, sandwich, salad and pizza stations are equipped with their own tray holders. Also speeding up the process are separate beverage and cashier stations.

A conveyer pizza oven with an exposed hood not only provides the cafe with a sense of living theater — it also expresses a fresh made image. To further promote a "country-fresh" and "homey-wholesome" image, a cornice/shelf made of wood matching the fixtures and decorated with ceramic tiles cuts the height of the space and carries decorative elements to reinforce the farm and fresh theme. Below, on the white tiled wall are mulberry colored menu boards also framed in wood. The deep cuff and beige colored ceiling "disappear" above. Straw baskets appear on flat surfaces offering breads and biscuits and muffins while also contributing an old-fashioned touch to the smart, contemporary setting.

Design: Dorf Associates, NY

103

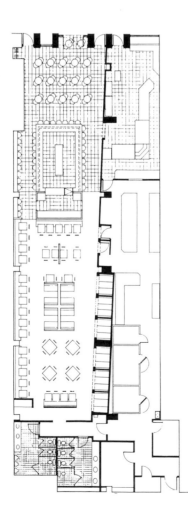

Design: Smith Blackburn Stauffer, Washington, DC
Partner in Charge: John A. Blackburn

THE AMERICAN CAFE

19th and M Sts., Washington, DC

Like most operations in this chain (see p. 54-55), the spaces are divided into three distinct areas; a cafe, a bar and a market. The exterior of this American Cafe on 19th and M Sts. in downtown Washington has two major entrances; one leads directly into the bar and cafe while the other offers direct access to the market.

The wall that bisects the market/kitchen from the cafe/bar also serves as one of the major design elements in the cafe/bar area. The wall has had areas "carved" out of it to provide a hostess station and also display cases. Some booths have been snuggled into the wall also for a "more intimate dining experience." "Boldly sculpted and positioned at an angle, this delineating object not only serves as a partition between two spaces, but is also used to control and direct attention to the mural at the rear of the space." Since the cafe/bar area is long and narrow, the mural — serving as a directional — draws the diners to the rear of the space. The mural features elements found in the restaurant and market and "local and regional icons are incorporated to identify the restaurant with its community."

The low, open bar of rich cherry wood on the front and wainscoting and its sleek chrome furnishings and stainless steel details is designed to be the center of activity of the cafe/bar. A star motif — the restaurant's logo — is incorporated into the design. One sees neon stars on the ceiling of the bar and in the market and, by means of projection lights, stars are projected on the walls, tables and floor — for dramatic effect.

To promote the flow from the bar into the market, the wall between the two areas is dropped and one can follow the neon stars on the ceiling or the black and white floor that unifies the areas. Neon also plays an important part in the interior signage of the market. Another design element that follows through is the stainless steel that appeared on the bar, it is also in the market where bands of perforated steel are used over the food displays.

The colorful fresh foods are used as the main focus in the market where they are presented against sharp white tiled walls and accented with the red and black of the American Cafe logo.

CAFE 180, MACY'S

Peachtree Centre, Atlanta, GA

To introduce the following group of cafes and informal dining areas in department and specialty stores we selected Cafe 180 located in the Macy's store in Peachtree Center in Atlanta. It was also recently declared the winner of outstanding merit in a contest conducted by the N.A.S.F.M. Essentially, this is a mini-food court in the department store and it features a gourmet food sales area and a cafe. The walls and counters are covered with white laminates and finished off with decorative natural wood crown moldings.

The curved glass fronted counters are contemporary in styling yet soft and gracious in feeling. Arches, outlined in black, appear over the wall cabinets to add another softening line to the design which is mostly crisp and straight-lined. The black accent also appears on the white tiled floor where black bands make effective borders.

The ceiling is blacked out and fluorescent luminaires provide the general light for the area which is also furnished with white milk glass shades that shield the incandescent lamps. They provide a warm glow over the pristine white counters and fixtures.

Picking up on the natural wood crown moldings around the square columns, light looking, European styled bamboo wood chairs are clustered around the white laminate tables — edged in wood. The black and white upholstery material is decorated with "X's" that resemble an over-scaled "caning" pattern.

Polished steel and satin brass are used to add gleaming highlights this handsome, neutral space.

Design: Regal Custom Fixture Co., Mt. Holly, NJ

CLASS

Perisur, Mexico City, Mexico

The Class Department Stores were created by the Paris Londres group of Mexico to express the growth of a new, affluent, fashion-conscious consumer in Mexico. They asked the NY designer, Andre Ruellan, to give architectural expression to that image — and to show how Class Department stores can be a new, upscaled, shopping experience.

The cafe, in the lower level of this Class store in the exciting Perisur Malls is given a dramatic sense of space in the three story well. The escalators, up and down, make for theatrical entrances and exits from the black, gray and white multi-angled space. The floor is laid with black granite tiles — gridded in white and patterned with white marble diamonds. The light looking tables

and chairs — also black — are grouped around in the octagonal shaped space. The shape is decoratively restated by the triple stepped cove that outlines the space and that is illuminated by fluorescent tubes hidden behind each step-up. This light, plus the general illumination provided by the ceiling fixtures above are reflected off the large mirror panels that line some of the angled walls. Mexican Colonial style cabinets and furniture serve as accent pieces as well as functional fixtures in the seating area where they also add a residential quality — along with some softening lines.

In an alcove — off to the left — there are illuminated glass encased cases that display the available foods.

Design: Design Team/Ruellan, NY

CLUB MONACO

San Francisco, CA

Club Monaco was one of the first "concept retailers" in Canada. They developed a highly focused and unique concept that combines product, packaging and overall presentation to form a highly integrated and comprehensive shopping experience. Club Monaco offers casual life-style apparel for men, women and children in innovative, and image setting stores.

The coffee bar which is an important design feature in the usual Club Monaco stores is here located along the outer curved wall of the shop near the entrance into the retail setting. Taking its cue from the European boutiques and trendy shops that cater to the young, the coffee bar/cafe concept is an important design consideration. Ace Architects designed this one for the San Francisco shop.

In keeping with the color scheme and the materials that are usually associated with the Club Monaco sophisticated/casual look, the lazy "S" shaped bar wiggles across the white floor banded in black and patterned with insets of gray. The light

natural woods that are used on the wall and floor fixtures are also used to face the sinuous bar sitting on a base of black and topped with a black laminate counter. Black vertical strips decoratively mark off the arced line. High wooden stools, upholstered in black, are pulled up to the bar.

The rear wall is mostly white except for a pier that is veneered in wood to make a vertical statement amidst the horizontal flow of the design. Oven and heating equipment are located under a shiny stainless steel hood. The cash desk, up front and nearest to the entrance has a display cut into it for an illuminated show of foods.

Blackboards mounted on the white wall under the bulkhead that is perforated with recessed lights serve as menu boards. The easy going, yet smart looking, coffee bar not only satisfies the Club Monaco customer but it draws in shippers from the mall.

Design: Ace Architects, Oakland, CA

MYER STORES

Adelaide, Australia

The HTI-Space Design International architectural/design firm was invited to "create a department store which incorporates the latest retail design trends from around the world and would provide Myer Stores with an image which is internationally recognizable yet still appeals to the consumers of southern Australia."

The coffee shop/cafe and restaurant areas of this award-winning store follows the design dictates that the architects/designers instituted on the fashion floors. They avoided excessive ornamentation, sumptuous materials and trendy effects in favor of a "comfortable environment" which they were able to achieve through the use of warm colored woods like oak and ash which

are indigenous to southern Australia. These materials were backed up with a relaxed and gentle color palette of sunny and flattering beiges and whites.

As in the rest of the store the designers superimposed "classically-inspired forms onto contemporary materials" like the metal fluting and trim that adorn the columns and the reveals. Each of the three different dining areas — from informal to semi-formal is "impressive but not intimidating — dramatic but not overwhelming." Each strikes just the right balance for this market and the needs of the particular shopper at a given time.

Design: HTI-Space Design International, NY

CRYSTAL PALACE & CAFE VIENNA

Marshall Field, Chicago, IL

In the complete renovation of the classic, landmark 1879 Chicago store on State St., the architects/designers were asked to re-create and expand on the "fin-de-siecle" style ice-cream parlour, the Crystal Palace, originally constructed in the 1930s. From its isolated location on the third floor it was moved to the larger and airier space on the seventh floor.

The informal restaurant is designed to seat 120 patrons and offers a limited and casual menu. Since the Crystal Palace was a Marshall Field tradition, the designers tried to keep as much of the familiar design elements of the original cafe as they expanded in the new location. It meant the arduous task of dismantling, restoring and then re-assembling the fabled stained glass panels that are probably the most distinctive elements in the design.

To make the space even more inviting, clear glass was added at the entrance, and to enhance the relaxed ambience of the cafe — an outdoor cafe was simulated. A striped pink and white canvas awning surrounds a central supporting column in the space and matching striped awnings stretch out from beneath the sky blue and white cloud painted fascia which is "daylight" illuminated by lights concealed behind the awnings. The palette for the area is pink and blue with white and pale gray used on the larger surface. Assorted turn-of-the-century decoratives and lighting fixtures have been added to let the "good old times roll."

For those in a hurry, there is the Cafe Vienna located on the lower level (Down Under) just off the Food Hall. This 25 seat coffee bar was inspired by the early 20th century work of Joseph Hoffmann and the Wiener Werkstatte. Most of the patrons who sit on the smartly styled stools and at the tables probably never even heard of Hoffman or realize that these items were "new" decades ago. The walls, the bar front and the floor are all tiled with small white squares and black squares are patterned on the wall floor is a style that is typical of the Viennese decorations of the 1920s. The neutral color scheme is accented with a gentle celadon green and a pastel terra cotta. Sophisticated down lights on long silvery stems light up the black bordered white counter top.

Design: HTI-Space Design International, NJ

BELK STORE

Southpark, Charlotte, NC

Located just off the food mall (see p. 220) is this warm and pleasant and very casual cafe. Wood is the prevalent building and facing material; it appears on the floor — on the frames of the booths and the service stations — as a cladding around the square supporting columns and even as an accent line cornice at the ceiling. With the natural brown wood color, the designers have used a mauve/rose color and a soft, seafoam green. The table tops are laminated in the rosy color which is also used as a flooring color in the food area on the right while the banquettes, booths and wooden chairs are upholstered in the green.

Planters are built in on top of the dual sided banquettes that angle across the cafe. The planters work as dividers and suggest a degree of privacy. They are filled with greenery which adds a residential quality to the space as do the framed graphics on the walls and on the columns.

BREUNINGER

Sindelfingen, Germany

The 200,000 sq. ft. department store was designed by the Walker Group/CNI and they were asked to produce "an ambience that is elegant and up-to-date — yet easy to shop; appealing to a more sophisticated and time constrained shopper."

Like the fashion floors, the Cafe is "modern and sophisticated — yet rich in variety." The materials and motifs that make the cafe so warm and attractive are those also seen in other areas of the store; the rich, natural woods, the smart and stylish accents of black and the gracious addition of curves and arcs to the straight contemporary lines of the architecture.

The shopper is invited to step into the semi-enclosed area to relax and sit awhile. The back wall of the banquettes that outline the periphery of the cafe also serves as the boundary lines and the

panels of "rain" textured glass that line up on top provide those seated inside some anonymity. Up front, an angled and well-illuminated case presents a variety of attractive food offerings and dessert possibilities and it also helps to establish the traffic pattern into the cafe.

The terrazzo tiled floors are a hearty rust color gridded with bands of black ceramic tiles. Satin finished black wood moldings and trim not only serve as the base for the case in the front but they also outline the wood veneered surfaces and the dividing half walls. The chairs are lacquered in black and furnished with light colored upholstered seat pads.

Design: Walker Group/CNI, NY

CAFE EPILOGUE

Pavilion Mall, Beachwood, OH

Taking on a European Cafe concept, the owners of a full scale bookstore in a speciality shopping center decided to expand their coffee service for the browsing book shoppers to include feature foods, imported beers and wines. Thus, a "coffee-house news-stand" was created in an 800 sq. ft. space set aside — with its own entrance — and with access to the books and magazines. "The challenge was to give this area its own identity while maintaining its relationship to the larger bookstore."

Within the limited space, the designers provided seating, a service counter, a pastry display, a work counter and a kitchen area. "The preparation area food display and coffee making activities are primary features of the program." The area is set off by a ceramic tile checkerboard floor pattern, black and white finishes which are easy to clean and colorful accents.

The sweeping soffit that curves over the counter/service area is finished in brick red and it carries a back-lit sign for the Cafe Epilogue which can readily be seen through the open facade on the aisle. The use of the simple black facade and the colorful sign set back inside the space "helps to make the store feel like part of the larger bookstore but with a direct connection to the cus-tomer."

The feature food offerings are chalked in on a blackboard set on a wall parallel to the opening; easy to see and easy to read. Almost at the window and close to the entrance is the brightly illuminated pastry display case to tempt the "non-book" shopper in the mall.

Design: G. Herschman Architects, Cleveland, OH
Photos: Stan Kohn, Cleveland, OH

ESMERALDA

Del Mar Plaza, Del Mar, CA

Tucked away at the rear of this wonderfully warm and animated book store is this tiny cafe that is not only for the convenience of the book-buyer who can't wait to start reading what they have purchased, but also for the stroller through the European-styled, multi-leveled Del Mar Plaza. The stroller has to be attracted by the charming and colorful murals that envelop the oak fixtured shop that is open for viewing through the large plate glass windows.

The murals are of fantasy figures and children's book characters executed in vivid colors and they move around the space leading to the mini-cafe area which is furnished with an illuminated case filled with baked goods and an oak counter/bar where freshly brewed coffee and espresso are available. In keeping with the simple and un-decorated look of the area are the bentwood chairs and the small round tables. Metal lamp shades hand down from the peaked timber ceiling of the book shop to send a warm and inviting glow out over the cafe.

If you are lucky, you may get a look at and maybe even be granted an "audience" with Esmeralda herself. She is the cat who "belongs" to the owner/designer of the shop, Richard Chase.

Designer/Owner: Richard Chase
Photos: MMP/RVC

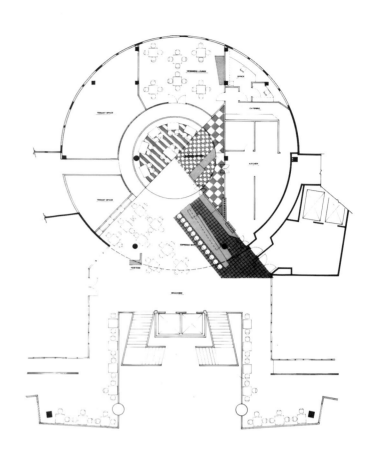

CAFE DESIGN CENTER

San Diego Design Center, San Diego, CA

Situated within the rotunda on the second floor of the four story atrium space, the design of the Cafe Design Center is tuned in to the taste of architects, designers and decorators who "shop" the San Diego Design Center. The layout is based on a series of interconnecting wedge forms since three different dining experiences can be found here; an espresso bar for gourmet lunches and drinks; an express counter for lunches and "picnics-to-go," and a more intimate lounge with waiter/waitress service.

The entry is open across the entire facade to integrate with the public space. The espresso bar acts "as a sculptural focal point askew to the symmetrical entry." It is composed of three dimensional wedge forms in polished black granite, brushed stainless steel on an underlit, etched glass top.

The express counter — located beyond the espresso area — is more "informal and whimsical." A black laminate counter in-

corporates bold geometric shapes in the colors drawn from the design center's logo. A fluorescent yellow string grid is stretched overhead and it is accentuated by the black ceiling above it. Located at the perimeter of the rotunda is the more elegant Designer's Lounge.

Basically, for all the areas, the color palette is black, gray and white — to match the overall scheme of the Design Center. To this is added bright and stimulating blocks and splashes of color. In obedience to the state's strict laws, BSHA was restricted as to their options on lighting techniques. For overall brightness, the designers used fluorescents and incandescents — both recessed and in shiny metal dropped fixtures —were used as accenters throughout the three dining spaces.

Design: BSHA, Inc., San Diego, CA
Dir. of Design/Interiors: Megan Bryan
Design Team: Melody Schumacher/Becky Zoni/Marie Avery

CAFETERIA, BECKMAN INSTRUMENT CORP.

Fullerton, CA

With the Cafe Design Center, on the previous pages, we introduce a selection of cafes, cafeterias and restaurants located in or as part of corporate headquarter designs — or other commercial spaces where food service adds a "perk" to the daily business routine.

Located in the corporate headquarters of the Beckman Instrument Co. is this handsome and stimulating cafeteria for the use of the company's employees and guests. In the sleek and sophisticated black and copper/brass interior, the menu includes a salad bar, shown here, that rests like a crown jewel on a jet tiled base and wreathed with light from above. Also available are selections from a deli bar, a specialty bar, a grill, a dessert station, a beverage counter, and one called "grab'n'go." Each service area is identified by the signage above it on the light washed, copper/brass laminate fascia that continues over the entire service line. The counters are white, black and gleaming with stainless steel and the warm metallic laminate used on the overhead fascia. Adding to the general excitement is the dark, mirror tiled ceiling which floats over the white ceramic tile floor.

Plants and live floral arrangements add a friendly and gracious note to the sharp, angular lines of the design executed in brittle and shiny materials.

Design: Patty Webb, R.W. Smith and Co., Costa Mesa, CA
Food Service: Art Manni

CAFE, WESTERN DIGITAL CO., HDQTRS

Irvine, CA

For the convenience of the employees of the Western Digital Co. this cafeteria was installed in the corporate headquarters located in Irvine, CA.

The natural wood veneers that cover the fronts of the food cases and the service counters are also used to sheath the supporting round columns on the white ceramic tile floor and also to create strong vertical design accents along the walls. The balance of the perimeter walls are flushed with a rosy/mauve laminate or with small ceramic tiles of the same color that are also used at the bases of the counters.

Accenting this warm color palette are bands of stainless steel and brushed brass. The two metals are also teamed up on the sneeze guards located all along the service line.

A dropped ceiling, painted pink, is outlined with a soffit of dark wood and it extends out around the perimeter of the room and angling forward for a dramatic effect over the open grill area. Dropped brushed brass metal cubes punctuate the space serving as air vents and light holders. In addition to the low voltage, high intensity lamps over the serving counters, brass and milk glass chandeliers, with light going up, provide the general illumination for the cafeteria.

Design: L. Jarmin Roach & Associates
Fabrication & Installation: R.W. Smith & Co., Costa Mesa, CA
Food Service: Art Manni

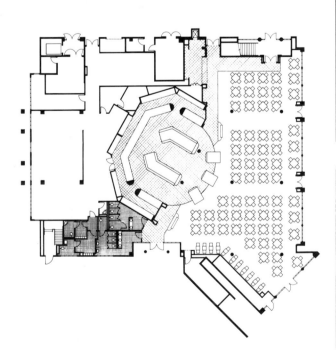

Design: Cole Martinez Curtis & Associates,
        Marina Del Rey, CA
Project Executive: Frank Goguen
Design Team: Martin Kessler/Joel Serafin
Designer: Elizabeth Koch
Photos: Toshi Yoshimi

PAVILION CAFE & CAFETERIA

Mattel, Inc., El Segundo, CA

The name Mattel is known worldwide as a leader in the design and manufacture of children's toys. The corporate offices are now housed in a new 14 story office tower and to satisfy the needs of employees and guests, two food service areas were designed.

On the main level is the Pavilion Cafe which is liberally sprinkled with color though it is predominantly black and white in effect. The ceiling soffits are bright aqua and — to match — the faces of the service counters set beneath the sweeping arc of the dropped ceiling are covered with a bold turquoise colored laminate. The lavender-to-grape colors are also used as strong accent colors to further the attitude of "a fun, relaxed atmosphere". Not only are the seats of the chrome framed chairs upholstered in a grape colored material, large diamond shapes decorate the long

side walls of the cafe. This focal area represents "a loose translation of the Hot Wheels logo," and the logo re-appears on the checked gray and white ceramic tile floor that defines the servery as well as other circulation areas in the building.

In the Cafeteria in the Design Center, the cool analogous colors are also used as accents. A saw-tooth wall with a stand-up counter attached to it combines an ultramarine blue with turquoise on a white background. The same, signature zig-zag line appears on the ceiling where the blue wire truss system serves as a dramatic ceiling track for the spots that warm up the white, black and textured metal surfaces below. White metal lamp shades hang down over the serving line which is also composed of counters angling in and out like the saw-tooth walls.

CAFETERIA, L.I. SAVINGS BANK HDQTRS

Melville, NY

Since almost 90% of the bank's employees prefer to dine on the premises, the cafeteria was designed, by the Spectorgroup, to be a "total alternative to the workplace" where the employees spend most of their day.

To accommodate the heavy traffic at specific times of the day, there is a three-way access from the servery to the cafeteria which can seat 300 and there is also an executive dining area for 30. The seating is laid out with tables that can seat 2-4-6- or 8 and thus lunch can be a "group meeting" or an intimate, quiet one-on-one.

Bright blue neon lighting outlines the geometric spaces in the cafeteria while also suggesting an up-scale, contemporary ambience that goes more with nouvelle cuisine than with corporate lunches. The geometric saw-toothing — or the in and out angling of the walls is underscored by the neon bands in the ceiling which, while "delineating areas of privacy," also respects the design of the building's exterior. To complement the cool blue light stripes on the ceiling, the upholstered banquettes are upholstered in a light cool blue color.

The savory island has a curving tray slide and cove lighting on the bottom of the rounded unit. The sweep of that servery bar is repeated in bold neon lighting above.

Design: Spectorgroup, North Hills, NY
Photos: Andrew Kramer

JERRY'S CAPPUCCINO BAR/CAFE & COFFEE SHOP

Pensacola Regional Airport, Pensacola, FL

A trio of dining experiences are laid out in the long but narrow, 9200 sq. ft. space in the Pensacola Regional Airport. Though the Pensacola area is rich in Victorian "stick-style" houses — there is also the strong influence of the Spanish-style houses built during the '20s when Adison Mizner was the leading architect/stylist in the area. According to J. Pendergast who worked as food consultant on this project as well as the liaison between the architects and Jerry's Caterers Inc. — "the Mediterranean Revival look says 'home' to most Floridians."

To unify the cafe servery, the bar and the seating area there is a full "vocabulary" of Spanish-style cliches in use; the red tiled roofs over counters and mini-bars supported by "massive" dark wood corbels; heavy timber beams projecting out from the bar wall to create a ceiling lowering trellis; Mexican green slate and hand made, baked faience tiles of various shades and tones of terra cotta and satin copper laminates that add a soft lustrous gleam to the space enriched with earthy and natural textures. To introduce the travelers, rushing by on the aisle, to the tranquility that lies beyond — a garden gate and a gurgling fountain bespeak the Spanish/Mediterranean/Florida look of the Jerry's operation.

The bar not only serves "spirits," it also supports a display of baked offerings, seafood and the cappuccino equipment. KRA "disguised" the 22 ft. long bar behind sand-blasted glass screens. According to Mr. Pendergast, "The screens let you know something is going on inside — but you can't look in and see someone drinking." The architects not only angled this bar — at a 45 degree — across the space — they used that same angular approach in laying out most of the shop's interior.

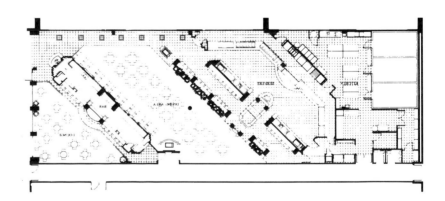

Jerry's Coffee Shop takes on the ambience and attitude of a 1950s diner. Jean Godfrey-June, writing in Contract Magazine, described the coffee shop this way, "Angles, spheres and boomerang shapes converge in a sea of patterned laminates, galvanized metal, neon, glitter sparked vinyl car stools and glass panels." The 800 sq. ft. space succeeds in recapturing the essence of the old roadside diners of the past in the newest and most exciting materials.

Design: KRA Inc., Atlanta, GA
Photography: Rion Rizzo Photography

FOOD COURT CAFETERIA, JERRY'S CATERERS

Melbourne Regional Airport, FL

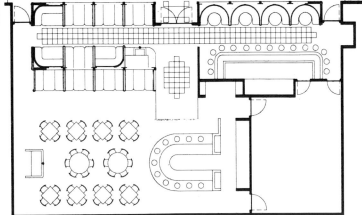

The cafeteria in the Melbourne Regional Airport is part of a food court which has been designed as a contemporary interpretation of "the Florida Style — an oasis in the center of an otherwise stark, contemporary building."

The servery was conceived, by the designers, as a stage and the stage is set and outlined with red oak millwork. Red Oak moldings follow the contours over the arched entrances into the seating area and the servery; they become the crown moldings atop wood gridded partitions and partial walls and they also encase sand-blasted glass panels which provide special dining niches around the open seating court.

Added to the white color that dominates the light filled space are cooling accents of aqua, blue and lavender and there is lots of greenery worked into the scheme. There are plants and bushes set into planters on the floor — in spaces between tables and there is an outpouring of foliage from the top of the partial walls that enclose the space.

The servery is designed in a staggered plan which allows the diners to make selections and move on to the cashier without waiting on long lines. The wooden grid motif appears in this area as well; on the doors in the arched opening and as a stepped window design in the beverage service area. These "windows" allow for "visual communication" between the servery and the circulation space. This is truly a garden of culinary (fast food style) delight.

Design: Taxis, Brad Schiffer
Photos: Rion Rizzo/Creative Image

BISON BREW/PUB

Berkeley, CA

We end this chapter with a stronger brew; the award-winning Bison Brew/Pub located in a unique, "megaphone" shaped building designed by the architectural firm of David Baker Associates. When the owner suggested that they do "something unusual — and have fun with it," he didn't quite know what an unusual and fun design he would get.

The lower level of the two story structure is surrounded by glass and the viewer on the street can look into the brewery, the kitchen, the bar and the dining area. One of the prize-winning attributes of the design of the 2225 sq. ft. space was "the fun delineation of the circulation plan" which consists of two mosaic paths that break through the black concrete floor. One is a straight line that leads to the food bar while the other one takes a more sinuous route to get to the bar.

In creating a "post industrial funk atmosphere," the designers used a mixture of rough building materials including — as seen in the bar — large steel panels bolted with industrial size bolts onto the base and topped with a contrasting countertop of mahogany and oak. The concrete cement counter top of the cappuccino bar is the work of Twyla Arthur who also created the circulation paths on the floor. This bar has a contrasting base made of bolted sheets of copper. A steel snake, by the sculptor Martin Metal, wraps its way around the railing of the stairs that leads up to the mezzanine. The interior walls are finished in a pale peach and silvery gray color. Overhead — lots is going on. An exposed galvanized duct pipe flows over the space interrupted by saw tooth shapes of metal screening that conceal the rows of low voltage lamps set behind them. A large triangular wedge of gray fills in one corner and it also carries some of the low voltage lamps that are used to illuminate the space.

When reviewed in SF Magazine, the clientele was described as "this is a college crowd — the average age is 23, and the culture you see emerging before your eyes might be labeled 'punk folk'."

In this architectural/sculptural/and art and artifact filled space where drinkers can actually sit next to the stainless steel tanks where their beer is being brewed, fun and freedom of art expression is what it is all about.

Design: David Baker Associates, San Francisco, CA
Photos: Michael Bruck, Berkeley, CA

CAFE KAVITA

Eaton Centre, Montreal, Quebec, Canada

The 700 sq. ft. area in the new Eaton Centre in Montreal is located in a prime, high profile site. The designers had to stretch the area to include display counters and a seating area for 30 as well as a prep area and a take-out counter. The emphasis is on a selection of coffees and the accompanying pastries, salads, light entrees — as well as wine and beer which are served all day into the early evening hours.

The configuration of the space was convoluted with a narrow 7' band along the mall end that ends at a small recessed alcove, "one of the prime design objectives was to fully exploit the potential of the expansive storefront (15' high x 58' long) and to minimize the special distinction between the leased and the public areas. A fully open front was achieved by custom designing and engineering a rotary closure system that pivots along a suspended axle. This striking element also serves as a signature design element — creating a theatrical canopy over the display cases."

The lofty space was emphasized by introducing full height glass panels, metal framework, color gradations on the background wall and high contrasting lighting effects. The designers opted for an inventive and dramatic mix of materials and textures; black polished granite, flamed terra cotta granite, rubbed solid

cherry wood, reverse painted glass, unfinished metals contrasted with satin brushed steel and "hand-crafted" paint finishes.

Gervais & Harding have created what they consider to be "the intriguing ambience of a 'taverne d'Epoque'" — a place of casual elegance.

Design: Gervais Harding, Montreal, Quebec
Photos: Andre Doyon, Montreal, Quebec

"Food was material to carve, mold into shapes, colour, turn to different textures. Cuisine was an art form for which enjoyment the epicure must employ all his senses; the eye to delight in the appearance, the nose to savour the aroma, the palate to experience the textures and juicy succulence, the ear to attend internally to the crispness of pastry, the crunchiness of nuts, the smooth frothiness of souffles."

Ben Johnson (1572-1637) on 17th cent. cooks

DAILY GRILL

Design: Steven Ehrlich Architects, Venice, CA
Photos: Mike Grosswendt, Los Angeles, CA

Brentwood / W. Hollywood, CA

Looking backwards to the great, comfortable, warm old grills of yesteryear, Steven Ehrlich researched the noted San Francisco grill, Tadich, and others of the period to come up with this neo-old-fashioned look for the Daily Grills.

The materials are contemporary as are most of the details except those like the black and white checkered linoleum floor and the dark stained wood around the bar, the service stations and the built-in booths — which are definitely "dated." The hemispherical milk glass shades rimmed and suspended with brass rods also add to the nostalgia that is underscored by the starched white tablecloths and napkins. Even being able to hang your coat and hat at your booth is a bow to the good-old-days.

In keeping with "tradition," the kitchen is open and viewable — creating a "theater of cooking" with a show always going on. The counter that turns a corner is topped with a gleaming metal laminate top and the pedestal stools, firmly rooted to the floor, also are a reminder of days gone by — the old grills and diners — as are the ketchup bottles and condiments arranged along the counter.

To serve good old American-style food, Steven Ehrlich created a "straightforward," inexpensive, durable and honest setting for a wholesome dining experience.

ARIZONA GRILL

Charleston, SC

What was a Civil War railroad station, circa 1864, was turned into an imaginative and exciting restaurant specializing in Southwest style foods by Chris Schmitt and Associates of Charleston, SC. The design team went back to the basics — to the original materials and construction of the RR station. Retaining the original color and texture of the brick piers, they were carefully restored and repaired and natural redwood bead board in fill panels were custom made to match the original wood. Overhead, the heavy timber truss pattern of triangles was exposed once the ceiling was removed.

To get the feeling of the railroad roundhouse that had actually existed in a space adjacent to the station, a large circle dominates the plan of the layout. The interior finish of the walls simulate red adobe — to go with the other Southwestern motifs such as the heart pine floors, the decorative "pony skin" upholstery, Mexican-style furniture and the American Indian artwork and artifacts. Probably the most striking design element in the Arizona Grill is the glass mosaic rattlesnake that makes its sinuous and "snaky" way across the front of the open grill and provides the visual excitement. The snake sculpture serves as the intricately mosaic patterned bar top for the patrons who prefer to sit on the high stools that are pulled up to the counter. The walls of the rest room cubicles that are centered in the rounded space are made of alternating squares of knotty pine which are stained a mossy green to match the table tops on the floor. The squares are "joined" with galvanized metal bolts and brackets.

Design: Chris Schmitt and Associates, Charleston, SC
Photos: Rion Rizzo, Creative Sources Photog., Atlanta, GA

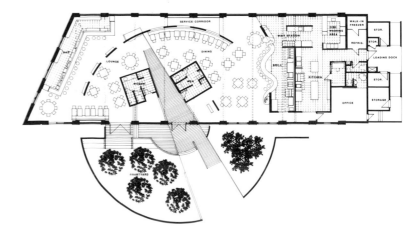

136

The lighting plan includes spot halogen lamps to highlight the tables and the artwork on the walls, and a lighting system that bounces the light off the ceiling trusses and spreads a warm general illumination throughout the space below. Above the curved walls that are so important in outlining the space, lighting bars have been provided to light up the walls and re-affirm their importance.

ZUNI GRILL

Irvine, CA

Way across the country to the West Coast and closer to "the source" is the Zuni Grill. With respect to the American Indian tribe of its namesake, the designers, Hatch Design Group, created this "cozy, up-scale eatery" in a desert, Southwestern setting. Giant faux granite blocks are topped with onyx-like panels to provide a dramatic entry into the space — "stimulating a cave dwelling found years ago."

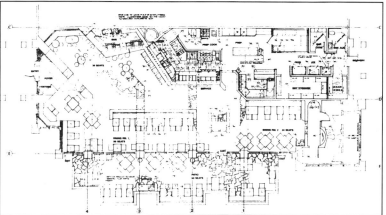

To further the texture-rich interior treatment and emphasize the "primal design," raw colored concrete floors sweep through the 4000 sq. ft. space broken up and patterned with irregular fragments of flagstone. The interior glows with warm, desert sunset colors that are applied to the hand weathered and textured wall surfaces that end short of the ceiling. Protruding beams of burnished metal layered across the space serve as the rough ceiling leaving the ductwork beyond well hidden. Throughout, jagged pieces of glass add yet another glinty texture to contrast with the construction materials.

Heavy woven fabrics are used for upholstery and stone flecked carpet is used in some areas while iridescent vinyl appears in others. The space is dimly lit by unique lighting fixtures of metal, mesh and glass — to enhance the dark, cave-like ambience of the grill. Halogen spots set in the ceiling turn the table top settings into inviting pictures.

At the rear center of the space is a long, multi-angled bar and the open grill that is highlighted by the drop lights that outline the serving counter up front.

"It is the unison of these natural materials with contemporary treatments that allows the restaurant its socially Santa Fe-an attitude, while at the same time, granting every patron a glimpse at the spirit of the Zuni people."

Design: Hatch Design Group, Costa Mesa, CA
Photos: Don Romero

AMERICA'S KITCHEN

Avenue Atrium Mall, Chicago, IL

Liberty's crown appears over the open exhibition kitchen/grill creating a dynamic, forceful and fun focal point in the L-shaped space in the Avenue Atrium Mall in Chicago. Tailored to the tourists who flock to this up-scale mall, the space is crammed with symbols and references to "America." The Statue of Liberty says "melting pot" and the whole idea behind America's Kitchen is to highlight American cuisine from around the states. Thus — the three-dimensional, ray-enriched tiara over the kitchen which is raised on a slightly inclined ramp — for better visibility.

To unite the space, a mural celebrating parades — especially American holiday parades — marches proudly around the open kitchen and on into the second dining area.

The color scheme of the space is almost all warm white, grays and black with some areas sheathed in wood. Part of the floor is natural wood while the mezzanine seating area is carpeted in rose/mauve — as are some of the seating areas in the dining room. The carpeting, combined with the dropped acoustical ceilings, helps to reduce the noise levels in the restaurant.

The lighting plan includes recessed ceiling spots and theatrical spots with barn doors to highlight the kitchen, the tiara and Superman zooming above. The wall murals are illuminated by the track system that follows the parade as it progresses through the space that accommodates 214 patrons.

Design: Aumiller/Youngquist, Mt. Prospect, IL
Photos: Phil Valasquez

ZAROSTA GRILL

Oakbrook, IL

"We wanted to bring the kitchen and the dining room together," says Keith Youngquist of the design concept behind Zarosta Grill. It is a theatrical experience with its wide open food preparation area spotlighted in the design layout.

The space is long and narrow — 45' x 85' and to make the "theatrical stage set for food," the designers put the entire food presentation area — the kitchen, rotisserie, pizza oven and bar — along the whole right side of the restaurant with the patrons seated along the opposite side. As if to differentiate the logitudinal space even more, a large metal duct runs down the center between the two areas. "Usually, when a finished ceiling isn't put in, the exposed unfinished ceiling is painted all black to conceal it as much as possible. Here we didn't hide it but painted it all white and used it as a reflector." Some of the reflected light comes from the frisbee-like shades on the pendant lamps that drop down from the ceiling to also provide the ambient downlighting. Above the all-important counter top, on the right side of the room, low voltage fixtures equipped with theatrical style barn door flaps are affixed to the truss system.

Faux marble finished octagonal columns are combined with natural oak floors, white painted brick partitions and banquette enclosures, and the high-tech pizzazz of shiny galvanized metal ducts and brushed stainless steel exhaust hoods and service units.

Design: Aumiller/Youngquist, Mt. Prospect, IL

FIREWORKS

This project is part of a new, night-time, entertainment theme park called Pleasure Island which is located next to Disneyworld in Orlando. The area is created around the mythical misadventures of a Capt. Merriweather Pleasure. "To this end, the plan of Fireworks is organized around the remains of blast bunkers built of used brick surrounding a steel and wood deck mezzanine. The detailing of the structure uses the vocabulary of open steel trusses and lattice columns to imply the archaeology of the myth. All of this culminates in the distorted ruins of the old watch-tower which becomes a 'chandelier' in the 35 ft. space."

Throughout, industrial materials are used; the floor is treated and block pineWS with brick pavers in the traffic areas and as a border for the black carpeted areas. Exterior grade corrugated metal walls are partially concealed by a pattern of acoustical panels covered in natural burlap and the walls have a wainscotting of black and yellow diagonally striped laminates.

A "roadhouse bar" that seats 100 is adjacent to the 300-seat, family style barbeque restaurant and here, too, the materials are "factory" related and totally eclectic.

Industrial lighting is used throughout with colored gels used to accent a collection of fireworks dummies. Neon is used for sculptural details as well as signage and as a "reminder of the mythical factory's earlier conflagration."

Design: Meisel Ltd. Associates, Chicago, IL
Contractor: Capitol Construction Group, Inc.
Photos: Erin L. O'Brien Photography, Cape Canaveral, FL

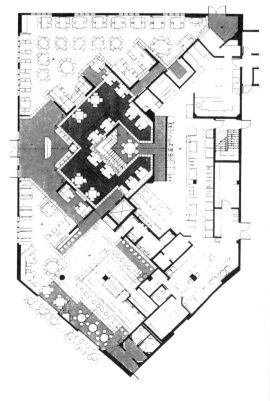

Design: Concept: James A. Bird, founder
Food Services Design: Douglas Kimura,
Bellevue, WA
Photos: Karl Bischoff, Seattle, WA

JUNGLE JIM'S

Orlando & Church St. Station, FL

Jungle Jim's is a labor of love — and "children" of all ages who go to a Jungle Jim Restaurant love being there. It is a fun and fanciful place with an extensive menu of all-American favorites plus South of the Border specialties served in an ambience that is a "tropical/urban jungle." On p. 144 are some views of the Orlando operation and on p. 145 is the new Church St. Station Jungle Jim — also in Florida.

Animals, gaily painted and patterned appear everywhere in the neon splashed space. Elephant "legs" become bar stools and also serve at the high pedestal tables in the dining area. A multi-colored, corrugated metal fascia runs along over the booths and it is finished with a wide crown molding that is even more

flamboyantly colored. Mache animals that might have stepped off vintage carousels are treated to outrageous colors and they now strut between tables and booths or stick out their necks amid the air ducts that criss cross overhead.

The polychrome explosion is even more pronounced at the Church St. Station location where a pair of iron lattice electric poles make a mighty duo in the middle of the space. They carry "high tension" wires down the length of the restaurant under the blue violet ceiling. The hot pinks, cerises, violets and acid greens are intensified by the gel filtered lights that fill the space with brilliant shocks of bright color and intensify the sense of excitement that is part of the Jungle Jim mystique.

ED DEBEVIC'S SHORT ORDERS DELUXE

Chicago, IL

*Design Concept: Richard Melman, Lettuce Entertain You
Enterprises*
Architect/Designer: Bill Aumiller and Spiros Zakas

Synonymous with the '50s diners is the ficticious character Ed
Debevic. Each Ed Debevic "diner" that opens across the land —
and even in Japan — is "a naugahyde and formica tribute to this
country's lost blandness."

Richard Melman is the guiding genius and creator of the
mythical Ed and as "Ed" himself tells you — "those of you
fortunate enough to have been in Talooca, IL around 1952
probably remember Lill's Homesick Diner on Highway 50. The
Homesick was everything a diner aught to be." So is Ed Debevic's
"classic" menu of '50-ish meat loaf, french fries, home-made
chili, fresh made hamburgers and "home baked" pies and cakes.

The restaurant, in Chicago, was the first of the ever spreading
Ed Debevic's. The '50s style decor is bright and gaudy, yet cheap
and does occasionally border on "bland. The chrome tables are
topped with marblized formica and the vinyl upholstery salutes
the flag — plus a lot of other flags; red, blue, black, gray, brown
and beige. A total mishmash of unmatched pieces are surrounded
by the colorless walls that are relieved by old-time signs and
artifacts. Ceiling fans spin around overhead while underfoot the
asphalt vinyl tiles are checkerboarded in black and green or black
and brown. The long service counter is faced with black and gold
veined formica as are the table tops that are spaced between the
chanel upholstered, blue vinyl booths. The ceiling fixtures are as
'50ish and it gets as are the diamond pattern embossed metal
panels on the kitchen wall.

Each Ed Debevic's is different, but each is the same; the '50s
revisited as a time of innocent enjoyment and food like mom
made — if she worked in a diner.

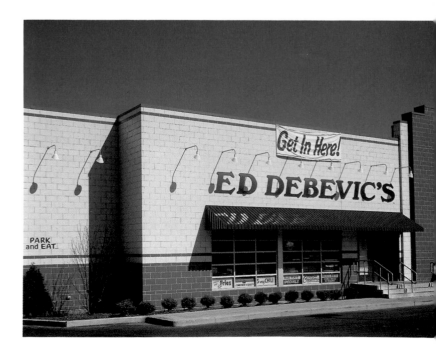

Design: Taxis Architects, Miami, FL
Photos: Rion Rizzo, Creative Sources Photography, Atlanta, GA

JERRY'S DINER

Tallahassee Regional Airport, Tallahassee, FL

The diner in the Talahassee Regional Airport was inspired by the streamline moderne diners that rode the rails — decades ago. The concept starts out on the facade where the old dining car that was part of the train that toured the country is recreated in the busy airline terminal. "The diner is an effective billboard sized merchandising tool." It is colorful, well illuminated and the long band of windows are enough to catch the traveler's eye — and pique his interest.

As the patron enters through the stainless steel door, the nostalgia is further enhanced by a variety of special details like the authentic red monitor windows atop the curvilinear stainless steel tambour ceiling that complement the dining car atmosphere. As a counterpoint to the comfortable rolled and pleated upholstery of the banquettes are the hard surfaced, stainless steel edged tables finished with vintage laminate patterns.

The glass blocks that are introduced on the outside are used on the interior to separate the dining car from the horseshoe shaped soda fountain and the dining room beyond. The glass blocks, lit by neon, conceal the service area and also refer back to the red, gray and black striped carpeting on the floor.

The continuous cove lighting adds to the warm, friendly ambience as do the '50ish fluorescent fixtures that follow the longitudinal axis of the space. The finish of the materials used, the furniture and the fixtures — they all together achieve a harmonious and distinctive look for Jerry's Diner.

HOPPERS

Michigan Ave., Chicago, IL

Hoppers' Dining Car was created to seat 170 bar and restaurant patrons and the "dining car" seemed to provide the right vocabulary for the menu-style — and for the linear space.

The store front replicates a traditional train station concourse with painted steel mullioned windows and a large rolling entrance door. The "schedule pylons" are used for signage and menu information as they also form a gateway into the bar.

A four color terrazzo floor radiates out from the bar which has a black glass face framed in cherry wood and topped with backlit, pale green onyx. Overhead, a cherry and walnut fascia is detailed as a schedule board with train names lettered in gold. The Dining Car — like a traditional railroad car — has a vaulted ceiling and linear clerestory lighting. Here the cherrywood trim and wainscotting appear below the soft cream colored walls. The display kitchen has a classic marble lunch counter with adjacent diner seating.

Oscillating wall fans, brass luggage racks, white tablecloths and napkins, upholstered arm chairs, polished brass and opal glass fixtures are all part of the dining car vocabulary and together spell out a warm, comfortable atmosphere for Hoppers.

To provide the patrons, while dining, with the feeling that they could be in an observation car, a 10' x 5' mural with a scene of a Western prairie is painted on the rear wall to reinforce the concept.

Design: Meisel Ltd. Associates, Chicago, IL

SILVER DINER

Rockville, MD

A visit to the Silver Diner in Rockville is truly a step back in time. It looks as though it could be "the real thing" from the corrugated metal exterior, the red neon lines a-blazing and the streamline moderne entrance into the diner.

Inside the space is dominated by the long food counter faced with bright blue ceramic tiles. The counter is bordered with a black and white checkerboard design made of tiles — the same pattern also outlines and borders the busily patterned blue and beige tiled floor. Using larger scaled tiles, the black and white checkered design appears on the wall behind the counter delineating the chrome and stainless steel panels. The counter top of the diner is capped with a '50ish laminate "marble" and the chrome stools are upholstered in a serviceable beige color. The booths are also upholstered in the same beige fabrics and they are framed in natural wood.

The ceiling overhead is curved at both sides to suggest the period diner architecture. Here, cove lighting washes the arced ceilings while wall sconces, between the windows on the booth side of the space, add a friendly glow to the hard, shiny surfaces used in the Silver Diner.

*Design: Charles Morris Mount/Silver, Ziskind, Morris,
    New York, NY*
Photos: Doug Brown, Alexandria, VA

Design - NYC: Himmel Bonner, Chicago, IL
Photo: Scott Francis, Esto

Design - Los Angeles: Dwayne A. Mann, A.I.A.
Corp. Arch. MGRE, Joppa MD
Photos: Ron Soloman, Baltimore, MD

BOOGIES DINER

New York, NY and Los Angeles, CA

Boogies Diner is the brainchild of Leonard Boogie Weinglass and it is "modeled" after the Baltimore Diner where Boogie hung out with his growing-up friends. He and it became the inspiration for the movie "Diner."

Boogies Diner is a one-of-a-kind food and fashion emporium; the trendiest and avant garde fashions are teamed up with a traditional "'50s style diner" in a setting that is high tech and low tech — the farthest out with the most old-fashioned of looks. The diner, usually located on a separate level from the boutique but very much a part of it, serves "home style chili," open faced turkey sandwiches with gravy, french fries, counter drinks, cakes and pies.

In the NY store (upper left) the diner is located on a 6000 sq. ft. mezzanine and features a 1950's soda fountain/counter with stools, as well as upholstered booths that can, together, accommodate about 100 patrons. Black and white laminate table tops, brightly colored upholstery, corrugated glass screens, wall mirrors and a hysterical palette of avocado green, purple, red, turquoise and terra cotta create, according to the designer Darcy Bonner, a "futuristic tossed salad."

The Los Angeles store (on this page) which recently opened, shows yet another facet of the Boogies Diner look with a palette rich in purple, violet, red, blue, yellow, black, white, and gray. As in the NY store, the diner is located on a mezzanine level and it can seat 68 diners. The counter top is finished in stainless steel and metal molding strips finish off the wood enclosed booths.

The shiny air duct snakes its way out in the open across the ceiling amid the pendant milk-glass tubular fixtures dangling from the ceiling. In each of the Boogies Diners, the designers have managed to capture the spirit of the '50s — but surrounded with the look and sounds of today.

Marvin Rice, V.P. of Store Design and Construction for the parent company, Merry-Go-Round-Enterprises of Joppa, MD says, "By using arresting colors and shapes in interesting and innovative ways, the architecture of the space further reflects the fun, free spirited philosophy of Boogies Diner."

WATER GRILL

Los Angeles, CA

According to the designers of the 7950 sq. ft. "sophisticated supper club of the '90s" — it is "art nouveau — one step removed." The space is fashioned along classical lines with a splash of Hollywood panache of the '30s thrown in to create the ambience of "the golden era."

The interior is rich with golden wood paneled walls and flooring—accented with gold and purple upholstery. At the front end of the lounge, a handsome display at the oyster bar offers an appealing "menu" of fresh seafood. Further on, separated by a streamlined, ribbed glass window and curving wall is the dining room which combines areas of privacy with areas of exposure.

The high paneled booths provide the privacy in this area where gold and teal appear on the upholstery and the flooring. Limestone blocks of golden ocher tones, "built in fortitude fashion," bring elements of the architectural style of the building inside. Other walls are paneled with black and silver moldings recessed in stained aniegre wood with graining set in oblique patterns. The ceiling in the dining room is painted in an ombre design that goes from purple to teal and the effect serves as an attractive background for the luminous suspended glass fixtures. Towards the rear of the space, the exhibition kitchen is revealed — for all to see and enjoy.

Throughout, artwork is used for color accents and to promote the desired image of the Water Grill. There are views of Los Angeles landmarks and of the sea done in a bold palette and in modern decorative style. "Through its stylish display of rich colored materials, warm lighting and gracefully curved furnishings — sophistication abounds at the Water Grill" and the "formal yet intimate Bohemian approach to moderne design" makes this a space to see — and be seen in.

Design: Hatch Design Group, Costa Mesa, Ca
Photos: Martin Fine Photography, Chatsworth, CA

PUFFIN'S SEAFOOD & PASTA

Toronto, Ontario, Canada

Following up with seafood houses, we have this restaurant in Toronto that combines seafood with pasta in an informal blue and white setting. The ambience is easy and relaxed; white tiled floors, marine blue laminates and pastel coral accents are combined in the open space. The chairs are white upholstered in blue and even the ceiling — like the ocean deep or the sky — is a rich and vibrant blue. Flapping in the breeze across the ceiling and adding bold splashes of bright, nautical semaphore colors are the sails suspended down from the deep colored ceiling.

An open kitchen/service area stretches along one side of the space with foods presented on hot tables and in glass enclosed cases. The fascia above is decorated with gleaming copper cookware and a blackboard that serves as a "specials" sign board. A row of incandescent spots are set up above and angled down to light up the show of food below.

The dining area is given a ship-board feeling by the glass windows along one wall and the greenhouse of angled glass panels on top. The profusion of greenery adds a lovely note to the almost monochromatic design scheme. Giant photo murals of Puffins — for whom the restaurant was named — are on the rear wall of the dining room where they are well illuminated by a ceiling track that is lowered from the ceiling.

Design: Hirschberg Design Group, Toronto, Ontario

SHRIMP COCKTAIL

King St. W., Oshawa, Ontario, Canada

The client specified an open kitchen, an island bar and adequate seating — all in 3500 sq. ft. of space. To accomplish the feat, seating is raised up on a platform 36" high and the "audience" can now look down onto the "stage" which is the open kitchen — with some "asides" from the bar. A feeling of intimacy has been created by having the bar and the open kitchen so close to the seating. The open ceiling is set at maximum height and the patrons' attention is captured by the flowing line of stainless steel, pieced with outlines of sea life.

To greet the diner, up front, is a translucent sculptured mermaid atop a stepped divider and beneath the bold forward sweep of the stainless steel ribbon banner which is cantilevered out from the bulkhead and wall. It also conceals the track spot lighting that projects from behind it. Colored gels of light project through the sea-life cut-outs giving an additional prominence to the bar and the two six foot suspended aquariums located beneath the sinuous steel canopy.

"Carefully selected colors, finishes, lighting, and repetitive design elements marry the space together — as well as points of visual interest impacting on the entire space." Mirrors are freely incorporated into the wall areas "to call attention to different focal points" and to add to the visual flow of the space.

Design: Hirschberg Design Group, Toronto, Ontario

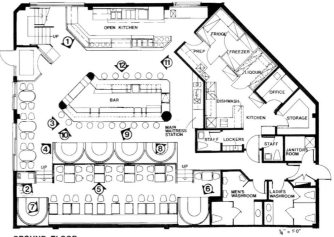

GROUND FLOOR

THE BIG SPLASH

N. Miami Beach, FL

The Benihana Seafood Emporium's The Big Splash does just that in a town where splash is all. The facade is brilliant with neon, pink walls and sharp red doors; inside the excitement really begins. "It was important to create a strong identity, an image that could be repeated, with details that could be altered to suit the location," said David Rockwell with regard to the designing of this 14,000 sq. ft. prototype layout.

The dynamic focal point in the design is the central piazza with the fabulous display of seafood. It is flanked by three foot high fountains and the spectacle is easily viewed by the "audience" that fills the 280 seats available. Overhead, the designers created an "artificial sky." "The ceiling suggests mystery and we wanted a strong horizon in such a large space." The actual ceiling was painted black as were all the mechanical systems and track lights. Dropped from the black void is a giant 2'x2' grid — painted light blue — and white canvas "clouds" billow across the criss-cross "sky" washed by the up lights on the columns.

Lighting is an important element in the design's success. In addition to the ceiling tracks above the grid and the up lights on the columns, red neon "paints" the walls behind the seating area and even the water in the large aquariums, built into the central piazza, glistens with light.

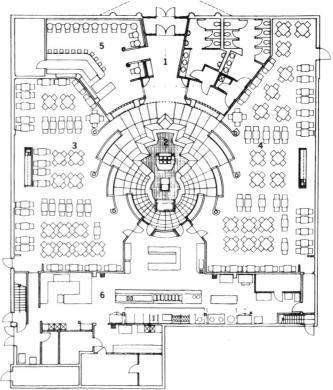

Design: Haverson Rockwell, NY
Photos: Mark Ross

CAFE SPIAGGA

Chicago, IL

Spiagga is a name associated with fine dining in Chicago and this is the Cafe Spiagga located in an office building in that city. It features Northern Italian specialties and here at the cafe bar the hors d'oeuvres are on display in brass mirrored cases. The bar itself is inlaid with panels of gray marble as is the bar top — framed in black lacquered wood and detailed with brass nail heads and foot rails. The black and brass combination continues as a square motif over the illuminated food cases and running as a fascia up to the ceiling — are translucent, back-lit panels framed in black. Ringing the curved bar are a series of frosted glass globe lights in brass fixtures suspended down on black pipes. To break the otherwise neutral color scheme, the textured walls are painted a salmon/coral color.

The emphasis here is on food temptingly arranged in cases — reflected in mirrors for total viewing — and beautifully illuminated to show off the colors and textures of the foods being offered.

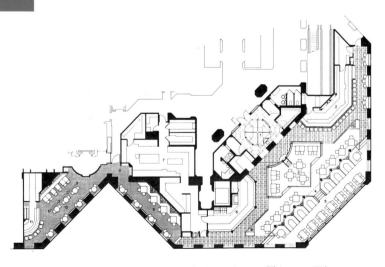

Design: Meisel, Ltd. Associates, Chicago, IL
Photos: Barry Rustin

Design: Hatch Design Group, Costa Mesa, CA
Photos: Milroy/McAleer

I CUGINI

Santa Monica, CA

"Inspired by timeless Italian design, I Cugini Ristorante is a feast for all the senses." The designers balanced the traditional styles and decorative motifs with the fast paced life styles of today. Marble, terrazzo, scrolled iron work, and heavy woven fabrics — in tones of cream, black and russet — "evoke a historical quality which is updated with contemporary overtones evident through various faux finishes resembling stone, hand-textured walls and granite." To break from a too formal look and to add some rustic charm, cherry and hickory woods are laid in a large scale parquet pattern on the floor. Also the exhibition style cookline which is attached to the bakery and the wood burning pizza ovens is brought into prominence in the design — "to bring the art of traditional cooking to the forefront." Artwork appears on the walls in Manet-style murals above the wainscotted areas that surround the serpentine booths. There are also painted details on the soffits and on the barrel vaulted ceiling.

During the daylight hours, the attached patio floods the space with light but at night the ristorante takes on a warm, romantic ambience. The space is illuminated by low voltage lamps and custom designed iron and alabaster chandeliers.

For those patrons who just can't get their fill of I Cugini fare, there is an attractively designed and stocked Gastromia/Alimentari attached to the restaurant. The diners can take home prepared and packaged specialties of the house.

GROTTO

Houston, TX

The Grotto is a multi-prize winning Italian-style restaurant located in Houston. Working with the owners of the Highland Village S/C, the designers transformed a former market into a "casual and energetic alternative for the city's youthful, fun loving restaurant crowd." The architects/designers were also able to integrate the exterior of the Grotto with the other shops in the center.

The focal point of the 3500 sq. ft. space is the rustic style, wood burning pizza oven and the counter/bar that surrounds it. This is where the action is — the theater — the drama of food being prepared. The high stools at the counter provide the best seats in the house. For those seated at the tables that abound on the hard, industrial floor — they too are surrounded by theater. A custom mural by Anderson Par wraps around part of the space with a bright, bold, and lighthearted salute and celebration of Neapolitan foods and Italian wines.

"Central to the design concept was the incorporation of authentic folklore motifs and objects of art from the Bay of Naples." Some can be seen mixed in with the bottles of wine stacked up in tiers of wooden cubicles on the wall behind the pizza oven — like a background for it. It takes a step ladder to reach the uppermost levels of wines and displays.

Blue neon washes the raised ceiling and miniature, high intensity lamps hang down around the bar to highlight the food preparation and service. The murals are illuminated by recessed spots set before them on the lowered bulkhead. Old fashioned fans turn about overhead adding a slight breeze — but a lot of atmosphere. This is "a true Neapolitan bistro — lively and authentic."

Design: Kirksey-Meyers Associates, Houston, TX
Photos: Hickey Robertson, Houston, TX

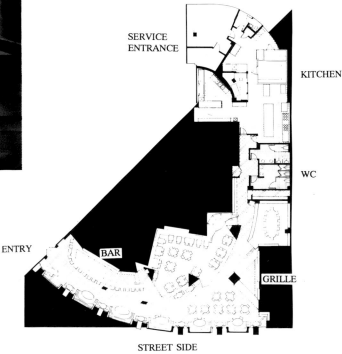

Design: SRK Architects, Philadelphia, PA
Photos: Matt Wargo, Philadelphia, PA

SERVICE
ENTRANCE

KITCHEN

WC

ENTRY   BAR

GRILLE

STREET SIDE

MARABELLA'S POMODORO

Philadelphia, PA

The restaurant is located in a building that was built in the 1960s with oddly configured spaces; there is an arc at one side and garage ramps through the back. Because of the numerous renovations on this structure it had become a space with assorted areas of varying ceiling heights — all of which now had to be organized into an inviting full service restaurant.

The highest ceiling height creates a "towering entrance" into the bar and then as the ceiling height becomes progressively lower — the dining spaces become more and more intimate. "Shaped low walls and soffits were utilized to give visual keys to the different sections of the restaurant without blocking the natural light and views." To create a sunny Mediterranean ambience the designers used quartz halogen, low voltage fixtures and neon.

Architectural surface materials of rough slate, zinc plate and quarry tiles were used to keep the maintenance simple — to help define the different spaces — and add to the feeling of being out-of-doors. Food is presented, up front, on the bar — as an overture to the dining experience that is to follow. In the dining area, wine bottles are laid on shelves built into the walls where they are not only available on order but they add to the decor and theater of the sunny and simple setting.

Design: Matarazzi Associates, San Francisco, CA
Photos: Russell Abraham

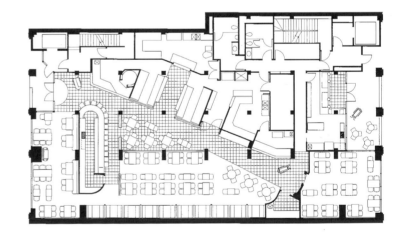

PALIO D'ASTI

San Francisco, CA

The 6800 sq. ft., full-service restaurant was designed by Matarazzi Associates to interpret the spirit of Palio D'Asti — a medieval festival annually held in the Italian city of Asti — from where the owners originally came. Using the closely spaced large columns and new seismic braces, which other possible restaurant tenants had considered a liability, as a starting point, the designers used them "to invoke a dramatic progression through the restaurant with a central diagonal axis gently winding through the columns in the manner of a medieval street." The "street" is paved with tiles set on a diagonal axis from the entrance and the curving path

is restated in the sweep of the dropped ceiling which is cut away to reveal the midnight blue painted ducts and actual ceiling construction above. The columns were stripped of their thick plaster furring which not only made them less imposing — the rough, sand-blasted concrete texture adds an "archaeological quality" to the setting.

The dining area is focused on the exhibition kitchen which includes pasta, dessert and pizza "shops" on one side of the "street" — to continue the medieval street imagery. Specially designed carts carry selection of antipasto as they circulate through the area. The carts are equipped with revolving mechanisms which bring different dishes up to the seated patron's eye level.

Throughout, Palio symbols and motifs appear in the design; wavy soffits of dark green, accent light crenulations, patterned banners associated with the Palio processions, custom lighting and sophisticated cherrywood woodworked details. The lighting is warm and intimate and though the design is contemporary, there is a feeling of antiquity in the total ambience. The Palio D'Asti lives on — in the '90s in San Francisco.

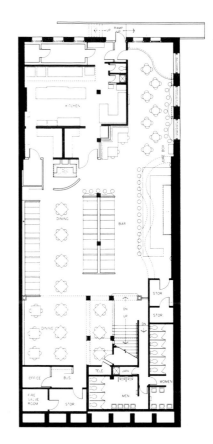

MEXICALI CAFE

Larimer Sq., Denver, CO

The Mexicali Cafe is located in the basement of a historic building in downtown Denver's handsomely revitalized Larimer Square. With the ever-increasing popularity of things Southwestern — and our natural relationship with our neighbors South-of-the-border — it was determined that a Mexican food restaurant could succeed in this space where other restaurants had failed. The theme came from the owners who envisioned a legendary character, Mexicali Sally, who drove her 1947 Cadillac throughout the Southwest opening restaurants featuring authentic and traditional Mexican fare.

The restaurant's bright colors, accessories and clever interpretation of the Mexican atmosphere "recalls the liveliness of a fiesta celebration" and Mexicali Sally's '47 Cadillac is emblazoned on one side wall as a focal point — and a trophy.

To get the diners down to the restaurant, a taco bar and display cooking, tortilla maker were situated up front — at street level — at the entrance to the Cafe. The potential patron then has only to follow the colorfully painted steel streamers down the stairwell to find the brilliantly polychromed dining room.

The lower level is finished with stamped, galvanized sheet metal which is used to wrap around the structural columns and atop the seating area partitions. More painted steel streamers festively wave over the bar to suggest the bright streamers associated with Mexican fiestas.

This restaurant recently won an award for new restaurant design in a competition conducted by Monitor. The judges felt that "the cafe's intriguing entry keeps the customers interested and the good use of colors and materials draws the customers in."

Design: Semple, Brown Roberts P.C., Denver, CO
Photos: Andrew Kramer, Boulder, CO

Design: Habitat, Inc., Tempe, AZ

THE DEPOT CANTINA

Tempe, AZ

Another Mexican fiesta is going on at the Depot Cantina — a 17,000 sq. ft. restaurant located in Tempe, AZ. Here, the designers aimed at creating an authentic Mexican street environment — "to replicate the flavor, color and natural ambience of vendors in a Mexican village setting by capturing the 'flavor' of Mexico through the use of festive colors, unexpected accessories and props and food items used in preparation for the foods sold."

The space combines high tech materials with what seems to be the gleanings from second hand shops, junk-yards and display prop houses. Humor is evident throughout in the selection of the custom props and decorative and architectural features. The concrete floor is inset with irregular pieces of flagstone and it looks as though kids, chickens and even adults raced across the concrete pavement before it had dried leaving their imprints and tracks. The ceiling fans are made of broomsticks and broken oars while the main chandelier is a fantasy constructed out of 1200

Mexican beer bottles. Display props include a "license plate bowl," shipping boxes and crates, blankets, foods and spices and hand lettered signs. Murals include life-size Mexicans standing about watching the "gringos" go by. A motion detector device enables the "eyes" on the dimensional heads on the painted bodies to "follow" the patrons going in and coming out.

Of special interest and value to the design is Tarchita's Tortilla stand located up front which presents a bounty of foods available beyond. Leaning out of an open window — watching the stand — is a life-sized, soft-sculptured figure.

The Depot Cantina also won an award in the Monitor competition. The judges liked the imaginative use of the assembled odds and ends and that the designers "created an off-balance, yet remarkably authentic environment." "It was like building a pyramid out of little pieces."

JOYCE CHEN

Boston, MA

The owner — recently returned from the courtyard gardens of Suzchow and much impressed with what she had seen — wanted that feeling re-created in the 7500 sq. ft. space in the new Transportation Building in downtown Boston. The design had to accommodate a 150 seat dining room, a buffet serving counter, a lounge and an all-important express take-out area.

A circuitous tile walkway wends its way through the restaurant and the occasional rails to either side suggest a footbridge that might gently arc over a stream or pool. According to the review of this restaurant in Restaurant/Hotel Design International, "It cuts the main dining room into two intimate spaces — runs past a free standing buffet and wends around to the lounge."

To affect the desired look, the designers combined traditional Chinese architectural motifs and structural elements with many contemporary materials and finishes. Under a ceiling painted sky blue and surrounded by walls tinted a gentle terra cotta color to simulate a garden's enclosing walls, stands a pavilion capped with a pagoda roof all made of plywood and plaster. Leslie Saul, the project's principal, incorporated projection lights that throw light pictures of bamboo plants on the walls.

In an area apart is the Express Take-Out counter which is attended by a magnificent 60' dragon brilliantly painted red, green and gold. The space is almost all black and white tiles and the angled counters are capped with bright red laminates. From outside, the dragon is on view.

According to Linda Lee Moore, who wrote of Joyce Chen in Restaurant/Hotel Design International, "Overall, color plays an important role in the design scheme. In the dining area, carpet, tiles and wall coverings are keyed to the earthy colors found in a garden. The same palette is used in the lounge — but in richer hues for added excitement." As Leslie Saul explains it, "the colors get progressively brighter as people move from the dining room to the bar to the take-out."

Design: Dean Tucker Shaw, Boston, MA
Photos: Warren Jagger, Providence, RI

Design: Mesher Shing & Milton, Seattle, WA
Photos: Dick Busher

RIKI-RIKI

Kirkland, WA

Riki means power in Japanese — and you get a double dose of power at Riki-Riki, a 3000 sq. ft. storefront location in a large urban shopping center. It's fun — it's upscale — and it's got lots of action crammed into the open kitchen — the sushi bar and the open seating as well as the tatami rooms.

"The design concept was an open restaurant plan using the sushi/display island as a focal point — and as a dividing element between the dining spaces." Because they need no windows and privacy is not the main objective, the tatami rooms, with movable partitions between them, were located at the end of the space. The black and white terrazzo floor is inlaid with white stones to represent a pathway that leads through the space which is finished with natural wood. To "represent nature" in the design there are the rough edges around the maple wood sushi bar top and the round columns between the tatami rooms. To suggest the more traditional forms and materials found in Japanese architecture, the designers used corrugated plastic as shoji screens and a pitched metal corrugated roof over the sushi counter.

The L-shaped counter can seat nine and they have an unhindered view into the open kitchen. The counter top is quite unique; it is made of a split maple tree trunk with the rough edge facing the diner. The top is inlaid with cherrywood for contrast.

For color and shock in this almost all-wood environment it is left to the murals that cover the walls like graffiti — above and below the chair rail. The theme is "manga" which is the highly popular comic strip form of entertainment in Japan. Three color schemes are interwoven with the comic strip characters; a yellow background on the exterior wall; periwinkle on the core walls, and a bright yellow/orange in the tatami rooms.

The custom designed light fixtures "are symbolic of shapes found in the Japanese culture." Low voltage lamps are used to accent and provide contrasts to the light level of the space. All lighting in the dining area is dimmer controlled.

CAFE JAPENGO

San Diego, CA

We conclude this chapter on theatrical dining experiences — with International flair — with the Cafe Japengo in the mixed use Aventine Complex in San Diego. The property's owner suggested an Asian theme and the designers came up with this contemporary interpretation of the Far East as it might be experienced by a latter day Marco Polo starting out from Japengo. "It provides an East Asian feeling without relying on stereotypes."

The 6000 sq. ft. space is divided into distinct areas though the whole space is as one in the gentle earth tones and the neutrals that are used throughout with gradations and variations in texture and pattern. An important feature is the sushi bar which seats 23. It is located up front and balances the lounge which is situated opposite it. The bar is faced with variegated blue tiles and capped with a natural wood counter top. A wood grid ceiling is dropped down over the sushi bar area to affect a sense of intimacy while the lighting for this "showplace" is contained in the wood enclosed ceiling over the work area/kitchen. The concrete floor that surrounds the sushi bar and the lounge — and the eight dining booths that are set side by side in two rows near the lounge — is textured with small dark gray pebbles. Squares of plain concrete are used to

highlight each booth and also to break up expanses of the textured concrete.

The seating area of the restaurant beyond is differentiated by the camel colored carpet patterned with squares of black — that all blends and meshes with the fantasy beige, brown, gold and charcoal gray landscape painting that envelops the space. It is a lyric and idyllic rendition of a Chinese painting. To protect the murals, Belgian limestone lines the lower part of the wall as a dado and a border of the concrete set with the pebbles, that appeared up front, serves as a "moat" to keep the diners from the paintings on the walls.

The monochromatic earthy color scheme is accented and delineated with crisp lines and shapes of black. Black grids serve as partitions as do the large shoji screens filled with a fine brass mesh material. Sharp brilliant light is provided by the low voltage lamps that are suspended down from the wires that cross over the restaurant beneath the blacked out ceiling.

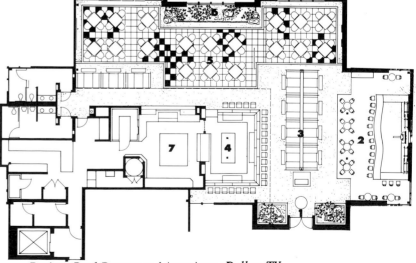

Design: Paul Draper and Associates, Dallas, TX
Photos: Milroy/McAleer

"You come in there to a warm, comfortable large room where a number of people are sitting at a table. You take whatever place you find empty, call for what you like which you get well and cleverly dressed. You may either chat or not as you like. Nobody minds you and you pay very reasonably."

James Boswell on London Steak Houses (1740-95)

FOOD COURT AT CAMBRIDGESIDE

Cambridge, MA

The center, a 1991 Mall Monitor Award of Excellence winner, combines an innovative shopping center with an office building, jparking garage and housing. It is pumping new life into the former industrial area sitting adjacent to the Charles River.

The prive focus of CambridgeSide is the galleria itself. This three-story regional shopping center combines the amenities of a festival marketplace with a fairly traditional shopping center in an innovative way.

The street level portion of the project is designed as an open-air "like" marketplace with specialty food shops, restaurants and cafes. The three-story high festival marketplace opens onto public parks at both ends.

The center's large food court is accessed via the Canal Park entrance. The seating area wraps around a curved glass facade with extensive views of the surrounding park, the fountain, and boats. Skylit cupolas above the two major courts create a visual focal point and retail beacons in the night sky.

What truly makes this project unique is that it has been designed and built to make the best possible use of its surroundings. Unlike many urban centers that are nothing more than suburban centers plunked down in the middle of a city. CambridgeSide looks and feels as though it really belongs to the neighborhood.

Developer/Owner: New England Development, Newton, MA
Architect/Designer: Arrowstreet, Inc., Somerville, MA

MC DONALDS

A&S Plaza, New York, NY

Located in the urban vertical mall in midtown Manhattan is the 2500 sq. ft. McDonalds fast food operation — the fourth McDonalds to be designed by Charles Morris Mount in Manhattan. This one is an explosion of neon, color and gleaming metallic surfaces. It also introduces some new design motifs that are sure to become signature design elements in future McDonald designs.

The structural columns that separate the three entrances into the space are clad with transparent, hand-cast, glass blocks which are backed up by mirrors. Each column is capped with a band of turquoise blocks.

Red neon tubes run behind the perforated, rotary finished, steel panels that face the black granite service bar at the end of the space. The bar is distinguished by the 6" bull nose edge. The illuminated counter serves to also draw the shopper over the tiled floor patterned in gray and white and bordered in turquoise and purple. Those accent colors reappear throughout the design. Overhead the ceiling is finished with perforated aluminum panels colored turquoise and finished to a mirror-like reflectiveness. This not only makes the ceiling seem to be higher, but the red and blue neon ribbons that wave through the space are reflected in the ceiling's surface. One of the blue neon bands leads the diner towards the main seating area which can accommodate 81 persons at counters and tables combined.

In the dining area the walls are color-filled "murals" of neon lights shimmering through the glass blocks that surface the walls. As in the second dining area (which seats 23) the table tops are white laminate and the chairs and table bases are black. The banquettes, under the glass block and neon walls, and the chrome based bar stools are upholstered in shiny green vinyl speckled with glitter.

The bright shine of reflected lights on polished and mirror-like surfaces — of perforated metals, glass blocks, vinyls and lami-

nates — plus the sizzle of neon ribbons floating overhead or broken into patterns behind the glass blocks all add up to excitement — and to fast food — spelled with a capitol F as in F-U-N.

Design: Charles Morris Mount, Silver/Ziskind/Mount, NY

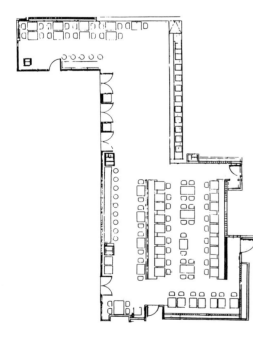

SHAKE BURGER AND ROLL

Ardmore, PA

The designer describes the 1768 sq. ft. burger/ice-cream "joint" as "The Jetsons meet Elsie the Cow." The "joint" has a '50s Jetson feeling combined with a very '90s tempo. The promoters wanted a '50-style "hangout" complete with '50s and '60s music recreated in a vacant Roy Rogers space and since the budget was very limited, the designer worked with paint, plastic laminates, linoleum on the floor — and lots of panache.

The two critical markets needed to make the place work are the young children and their mothers who come for lunch or after school snacks and the college students for the evening hour trade. The designer picked the Jetson cartoon series as the design concept since it was so filled with images and shapes that were popular in the '50s-'60s — and they are still around today.

The counter tops and table tops combine the irregular shapes and angular forms to resemble "cowskin" and the funnel shaped columns that support the amoeba shaped dropped ceiling look like something that has been cleaned up and transported from Flintrock. Here tungsten bulbs sparkle through the openings in the floating, edge-lit shape. This is what attracts the passersby who can see in through the wide open glass windows that surround the space. The columns also serve to frame the focal point of the design — the boomerang-shaped soda fountain with its neon-lit, "rock" shaped mirrors and corrugated fins — back up with natural plywood storage cabinets above.

The color scheme is quite neutral; in addition to the black and white the scheme includes camel colored naugehyde upholstery on bar stools and on the booths that hug the window line. The floor is laid with beige and camel linoleum squares accented with black and the major accent colors are the soft teal of the columns and the floating ceiling and the marigold yellow that appears on

the convoluted valence above the windows in the rear and on the squares appliqued onto the wall behind the soda fountain counter.

Design: Hugh Boyd, Boyd Associates, Montclair, NJ

KENNIES DINER

Bayshore Mall, Milwaukee, WI

Kennies Diner "creates a nostalgic return to the days of the Art Deco diners of the '30s" says the architect/designer. It is located as an in-line store fronting the main court of an enclosed, up-scale mall. Since it is not part of a food court it "necessitated a strong image so as to achieve an identity impact in competition with all the other retail vying for recognition."

To carry through the thematic design concept, stainless steel, neon and graphics were used. The menu boards and display trim items are all based on images of that period and the neon logo clock is another distinctive design element. The mall management allowed Kennies Diner to place several "theme-style" stools at the side of the front counter as well as an operational juke

box — all of which extended out beyond the lease space into the mall. The landlord also permitted the neon "item" signage that runs on a band below the diamond patterned fascia that carries the Kennies Diner logo in '30ish style neon letters. The same diagonal design, impressed on stainless steel, is used to face the front of the service counter — and the "diner counter" on the left.

The white tiled columns that break up the mall spaces are used here to define the "diner" on the left from the service area on the right. The rear wall of the operation is also finished with gleaming sheets of stainless steel.

Design: Phillip LeBoy Architects, Skokie, IL

HOT DOGS

Lower Broadway, New York, NY

This fun and frolicking Hot Dogs stand is about as "old-fashioned" as a brand new Hot Dog stand can get. It is located on lower Broadway in an area that is expanding with trendy clothing boutiques, smart, youth-oriented restaurants, cafes and coffee houses, record shops and street vendors selling all sorts of daring and shlocky fashion accessories. Aside from the colleges and the university nearby, this area draws students from all over with its street-filled excitement.

The simple, satin steel plated facade is pierced with multiple glass doors so that the whole space is on view from the street. The helter-skelter scatter of assorted colored ceramic tiles on the basically white tiled walls is repeated on the dropped ceiling with translucent panels of white interspersed with squares of red, yellow, green, blue, and orange. It is the same haphazard pattern only on a larger scale.

The service counter is faced with a diamond grid laminate of black and white and topped with a mottle green, black, and white Memphis-ian splatter pattern. Super-imposed are squares of light blue and avocado green. To add yet another pattern to the already pattern-laden space, the floor is laid in a checkerboard of gray and white.

The big news is the 75¢ hot dog and it is stated in red and yellow neon on the steel-covered air vent over the service counter. Outside the other specialties of the house are recorded in neon too. The other choices are noted on the black menu board, framed in gray laminate, situated over the yogurt machines. For those who want to "dine in" — it is stand-up only at a counter across the rear wall or at high pedestaled tables on the entrance wall.

Design: Evelyn Sherwood Designs, New York, NY

BLIMPIES

Houston, TX

The headline reads — "Blimpie is adding a few new ingredients for winning customers to the premier submarine sandwich franchise; cheerful colors, decorative flooring plus the creative use of accent light and glass." The new restaurant design coincides with the aggressive expansion plans of Blimpie to have 1000 restaurants by late 1994.

The original color scheme, inaugurated in 1974, of red, yellow and green, has been updated to make the restaurants "more cheerful and appealing." Customers are led to the expanded counter by white tile flooring bordered with red and yellow accents. The counter tops are laminated with a red, white and green material patterned with a checkerboard design and to draw attention to the Blimpies freshly baked breads, a green hood is used over the bread rack and the oven. There is lots of glass used

to open up the workspace and enable the customers to see the sandwich fixings — all fresh cut.

Most of the Blimpie franchise operations range from 1000 to 1500 sq. ft. and can seat up to 50. The new up-scale look plays up the traditional red, yellow and green, but adds lots of white to "reinforce the concept of freshness." Blimpie has also introduced a new line of "Lite" sandwiches and salads — in keeping with diet workshops.

Still in an experimental stage is The Freshery — a separate restaurant in the Blimpie chain that features up-scale gourmet salads, deli pastas, and fruit and vegetable salads.

Design: Joe Conza, Exec. V.P., Design & Construction

BOSTON CHICKEN

Boston, MA

Also tuned in to the new American health-conscious life style is Boston Chicken. In stores that are about 1500 sq. ft., rotisserie chicken is being offered along with hot vegetables and deli salads; the emphasis is on healthy foods, low-fat, well-prepared, appealing and convenient. The targeted market is "anyone who seeks a convenient and healthier alternative to traditional fast foods."

Though most of the restaurant's business is conducted in the early evening hours when people stop to shop for a nutritional and complete meal — to go, there are still those who lunch or snack during the day on the twice marinated and rotisserie roasted chicken and the accompaniments. Tables and chairs are provided in the beige, white and natural wood lined interior.

The floors are paved with beige ceramic squares inset with coral tiles that echo the color of the soffit that runs along over the long and angled counter. The food selections and destination markers are carried on the fascia in oak framed signboards. Wide swaths of oak edge the light laminated counter which is illuminated by the pendant lamps with brass metal shades. Spots on the ceiling track light up the signboards and recessed incandescents provide the warm ambient light for the seating area.

Prepared salads and freshly prepared foods are on display in large glass cases to either side of the glass protected steam table and near the order-taking station. Live plants hang from the ceiling to visually separate the seating area from the counter as do the oak separators capped with brass rods.

"We're trying to avoid looking like a fast food place — we're using materials that are not plastic." The new look is succeeding with young up-scaled professionals as well as in gentrified locations.

Dir. of Construction: Douglas H. Anderson

Design: Rockefeller/Hricak, Venice CA
Photos: Christopher Dow

SUNNY'S

Cypress, CA

Yogurt is not quite replacing ice cream as the frozen dessert of choice but it is becoming a more and more popular option for calorie, fat, and cholesterol watchers everywhere. It has come a long way from its "healthy" beginnings to now when it is fun and flavorful, delicious and available with dozens of do-your-own sundae toppings.

In Southern California where health-consciousness is a full-time preoccupation, Sunny's is a bright and sunny yogurt operation. In the 1230 sq. ft. space yogurt lovers are invited to build their own treats. The walls are painted stark and pristine white and super-imposed all over and around them are crayola colors in industrial finishes: red, yellow, blue, and green — the bright primaries. They pick up and reinforce the color of the toppings that appear in the center of the space within a glass and steel red "factory" with a peaked roof. According to the designer, Michael Hricak, the whole fun feeling is based on a factory assembly line. The patron picks up the cone, cup or container at station #1 then proceeds to station #2 where he/she fills up with the flavor or flavors of choice. Station #3 is the factory, previously mentioned, in the center of the floor where individual creativity and taste take over with the toppings. "The participation factor is what makes this shop stand out from the others. Customers don't just walk in and pay; they get to make their own creations."

Under the even- and high-level of illumination provided by the recessed fluorescent fixtures and the blaze of neon accents, the patrons can sit at the light-looking chairs and tables or at the counter near the entrance, on stools.

SUSAN'S OWN ICE CREAM

Springfield Mall, Springfield, PA

To create a new image — and a more diverse menu — for Susan's Own — a counter/ice-cream shop, the Office of Charles King was called in. In the square space allotted, the counter area was redesigned into a galley arrangement with the counters facing both mall corridors. The balance of the space was reorganized for more efficient stocking.

The counter is faced with white tiles and banded in black. It is bowed in the center to make a gentle transition from aisle to aisle and yet affect a long sweep of counter. Overhead on a hunter green fascia outlined in brass, the new corporate logo appears in neon. The forward bow in the middle of the overhead band steps down and forward to gain greater visibility from all sides and it is decorated with a row of neon-outlined ice cream cones.

The rear wall of the service area is tiled in white and also capped in black. Over it and carrying the brass framed signboards is a dark green area painted to match the fascia in front. Flavors of ice cream are on view on each side and the toppings are located, behind glass, in the middle.

Design: Office of Charles King, Philadelphia, PA

190

MINTERS ICE CREAM

Independence Mall, Kingston, MA

The ice cream/tropical fruit juice bar is situated, like Susan's Own, at an intersection of a food court — here at the Independence Mall in Kingston. This allowed the designers the opportunity for "unique design approaches." They reversed the conventional inward layout and eliminated the bulkhead and thus allowed "the front counter displays and back board signs to aggressively spring out into the open — and yet its rich color scheme warmly invites customers to approach."

The space is divided into four display counters by the five double arm arches that spring out from the back wall. Each outer arm is capped with a signage board and sandwiched in between the inward arced arms are the colorful, horizontal menu boards. The use of the electric blue arcs that extend forward effectively separates the ice cream operation from the fruit juice area.

In addition to the metallic blue of the arches there is the bright red painted arms and sign frames as well as the yellow of the signs and menu boards all seen against the white background. The long, angled counter is faced with a wood veneer and has a white tile baseboard that blends in with the flooring in front of it. The counter top is finished with a gray granite-like material and stainless steel and glass sneeze guards and display cases are arranged on the counter top.

Behind the wall, the storage area and office have been condensed and a mezzanine level was added to maximize the usage of the space. Transom windows, seen behind the long menu boards, help to define the space within the space.

Design: Tony Chi & Assoc., NY
Design Team: Tony Chi/Albert Chen/Rafael Caceres, Jr

GREAT AMERICAN COOKIE COMPANY

The Great American Cookie is becoming an easily recognizable and familiar sight in malls — in food courts — and even tucked in amidst fashion and specialty shops. The white, neon-lit, "Cookie Co." sign with "Great American" scrawled across in red neon is a beacon that draws cookie lovers to the curved glass display cases that are lined up over displays of made-to-order cookies and cakes shown in glass cases set within the counters. The counters are constructed of wood, copper and glass and usually finished with beige tile baseboards.

The copper/brown color scheme continues on the rear wall where a brown and white checkerboard pattern is visible at eye level. A wide chocolate brown fascia above carries the back-lit graphics which, in a way, serve as sign boards for the products on view below.

The stands will vary in size but are usually about 500 to 600 sq. ft. This is a franchise operation and quality control is guaranteed by having all the batter pre-mixed in the Atlanta based production facility. From there it is shipped by refrigerated trucks to the assorted stores, stands and kiosks. The employees are trained to measure out the right amount of batter so that the cookies and brownies can be baked in the ovens on the premises. That adds the sense of smell to the visual presentation in, and on top of, the counters.

STOCK POT

Westlake Center Mall, Seattle, WA

The main business of The Stock Pot Soup Company is to provide soups for the restaurant trade and for wholesalers to package for retailers. This outlet, in Westlake Center, is not only to satisfy those who prefer a "soup and" lunch, but to further promote the primary business.

Since the space is open on three sides and at the crossroads of several circulation paths in the food court, it presented many challenges to the designers. It is "difficult to establish a strong image and identity against a background of all the other food vendors in the mall."

The solution was to make a strong backwall that splayed out at the top to present as large a presence as possible. The angled forward panels are gently patterned with a design of "vegetable" colors "swirled in cream" — to reinforce the soup image of the company. The over-scaled, dimensional vegetables that are applied between the red and green menu boards serve as "icons" for the product and also to emphasize the concept of "fresh" in the "fresh soups." Six gleaming soup kettles are very visible on the counter to point up the variety and the importance of soup to the manufacturer. It also makes a dramatic impact on the shopper.

The bright green laminate covered counters and displayer cases project the "fresh vegetable" concept even further while complementing the prepackaged soup mixtures available for purchase. Red straw baskets hold the long French baguette breads that are sliced and served with the soups.

Design: Mesher Shing & Assoc., Seattle, WA
Photos: Dick Busher, Seattle, WA

UNLIMITED PASTABILITIES

A&S Plaza, New York, NY

The designers tried to recreate "a country kitchen — like Grandmother's cozy kitchen" in the sleek, urban, vertical shopping mall food court. The 560 sq. ft. space is all open and all the food preparation is on view to the diners in the food court.

Two white tiled service counters decorated with inset tiles featuring the restaurant's logo and black diamond shapes, flank the central wooden counter which is reminiscent of an old-fashioned butcher block or a provincial table. Behind a glass sneeze guard and topped with a glass shelf for additional display is an array of the prepared foods, pastas, salads, and such — all beautifully illuminated. The stepped white tile walls on either side of the space end in narrow dividing walls that frame the open kitchen beyond. The same tile design is used to finish off the rear wall which is also equipped with glass fronted wood cabinets, overhead — like in Grandmother's kitchen.

The quarry tile topped work island is on view behind the wood counter and the bottom of the island is made up of matching glass and wood cabinets for storage of components and packaged foods.

The changing specials are handwritten in chalk on the wood framed blackboard sign that is attached to the stainless steel air vent/hood that is suspended over the work island.

In keeping with the Italian cooking premise, decorative accents include sheaves of wheat, herbs dried and tied, strings of garlic and huge blocks of cheese which are all staples in the traditional Italian kitchen.

Design: Tony Chi & Associates, NY
Design Team: Tony Chi/Albert Chen/Rafael Caceres, Jr.
Photos: Dub Rogers

L.A. ITALIAN

Tyler Mall, Riverside, CA

Rust-colored blocks of marble face the angled counter/service bar and they are also laid on the floor of this mall enclosed space that is further warmed by the apricot colored walls and the recessed incandescent lamps in the ceiling.

What you see is what you get in L.A. Italian. The shop features Italian fast foods: pizzas, pastas, sandwiches, desserts, and beverages. Patrons place their orders at the display counter where the food is all attractively presented. Old-fashioned, white milk glass shades hang down from the coved ceiling over the service area to light up the foods below. A red neon ribbon runs along the fascia occasionally spelling out one of the specialties of the restaurant.

To add an illusion of depth to the long, narrow space, the entrance area is wider than the rest of the space and a wall of mirrors, on the right, reflect the wall on the left. Patron seating is provided with light chairs and tables pulled up to upholstered banquettes that run the length of the left hand side of the space. The banquettes are interrupted by black lacquered tray stands and trash receptacles that are topped with classic urns filled with foliage. Photo blow-ups of famous Italian statues, sights and landmarks decorate the wall over the seating. Up front — on the far right — there is a small counter with pull-up stools for additional seating.

The pizza-making exhibition, the wood-burning ovens and the espresso bar all add to the visual stimulation of the design.

Design: Karen Moncrief, R.W. Smith & Co., Costa Mesa, CA
Food Service: Art Manni/Jim Nocerina, R.W. Smith & Co.

PIZZERIA REGINA

Fanueil Hall, Marketplace, Boston, MA

The Pizzeria Regina was renovated recently and enlarged by 40%. Also included in the redesign of the space was the introduction of some new prototypical design elements.

The space was originally designed by the Bergmeyer Assoc. over 15 years ago in the landmark Marketplace at Fanuiel Hall and the spacing of the supporting Doric columns was, and still is, a problem the designers have to contend with. In order to update the look of the area and still be true to the surrounding space, the designers selected a neutral black, white and brushed steel palette accented with bold strokes of red.

Nowhere is the new design more evident than on the handsomely conceived sign boards that line up overhead over the long, narrow space. Authentic 1960 Cadillac tail lights in red add sparkling accents to the stainless steel, '60s-inspired fin shaped boards outlined with black and red. Red panels and dividers also serve to delineate areas of food presentation on the counter which is also finished in stainless steel with rounded surfaces, arcs and fins. The stainless steel is not only durable and easy to keep clean, it was used for its visual effectiveness.

One of the major operational changes that was made was to bring the pizza up front for display — and to attract the customers.

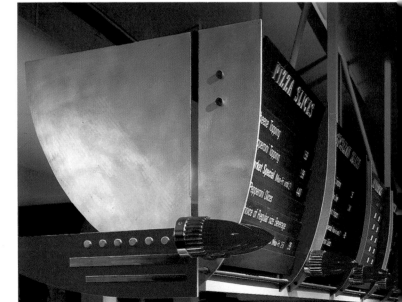

To make sure the pizza is seen to its best advantage, white metal lamp shades hang down from behind the white painted air ducts and focusable spot fixtures are attached to the back side of the lintel supported by the white Doric columns.

Design: Bergmeyer Associates, Inc., Boston, MA
Photos: Lucy Chen Photography, Cambridge, MA

Design: Planned Expansion Group, White Plains, NY
Photos: Elliot Fine Photography, NY

MAMA BRAVA PIZZERIA

Freehold Raceway Mall, Freehold, NJ

This prototype design was first implemented in the Freehold Raceway Mall, but with adaptations will be appearing in other malls and in downtown locations.

The image that was to be projected "through the special configuration, architecture and finishes was to be Italian" — in keeping with the cuisine — but also "contemporary." What the designers hoped to create was the kind of ambience one associates with small, side street cafes — cozy gathering places that are "typically Italian."

To get the desired effect they combined brass, copper, marble, terra cotta with traditional red and green, "materials, finishes and colors were selected with an eye to Italy's bounty and the warmth of the people."

A special grid is formed by engaged columns at the store's perimeter and floating copper beams which project from the columns and are connected to each other and the ceiling by brass elements. A curved soffit — accented with red and green neon streamers — curves its way sinuously between the copper beams and the ceiling above leaving behind a trail of shimmering reflections. Each copper beam is accented by a distinctive light fixture that also helps to define the circulation area. Each individual booth or dining cubicle is also defined by the spacial grid above while being illuminated by the pendant, metal shielded lamps.

MOZZARELLA DI BUFALA

Filmore St., San Francisco, CA

The designers took a run-down, boarded-up store front and turned it into the slick, but friendly, Mozzarella Di Bufala — a place that bakes and sells only pizzas and salads. The emphasis is on take-out and fast delivery though seating is available.

The space runs 99' deep and is only 15-1/2' at its widest with a ceiling height of 12'. To complicate matters — there are structural columns every 13' on center. The designers set the pizza ovens in the rear half of the space with a counter area for pick up and used the front part of the space for table service seating. Since the owners are Brazilian, the designers took their design cues from that and created "an open, airy, sunny, and spare atmosphere punctuated with Brazilian touches of color and the wave pattern of the walkway at Copacabana Beach in Rio de Janiero."

The columns are used to define the bays for seating — creating a sense of privacy. To emphasize the bays, low partitions were added that connect the columns to the exterior wall. Both the columns and the partitions are clad in an inexpensive stain-grade plywood that was left natural and only treated with a clear sealer. As one moves further into the pizzeria, the height of the low partitions increase till the highest partition — at the third bay — hides the busy kitchen.

Light boxes are worked into the partitions to up-light the colorful sculpted waves that are attached to them. The wavy line is also repeated above the framed mirrors on the wall and boldly interpreted in black and white on the concrete floor.

At the end of the seating area is a bar/counter with a display of specialties. Contemporary pendant low voltage lamps serve as accent highlighters.

People come to Mozzarella Di Bufala for the gourmet pizzas — and the feeling of carnival that fills the space.

Design: Calvin Lau Designs
Design Team: Calvin Lau/Visnja Batkovic/Noel Remigio
Photos: Michael C. Lewis

THE FOOD EXCHANGE TERRACE

Ilford, London, England

We open this section devoted to food courts with this recently opened food court designed by the John Herbert Partnership of London. The Exchange Food Terrace is located on the upper level around the balcony edge with views into the central concourse atrium. The space is light and airy — flooded with natural light from the domed skylights by day and from the neon strip lighting within the domes at night.

There are nine separate food vendors here and they are located under a vaulted arcade along one side of the Terrace. They are separated from each other by stepped wood capped walls "which allow good visibility into each and provides an overall architectural framework to the whole arcade." An overall discipline is maintained by the use of standard tiled format for both signage and the kiosks. For each stand "identities have been developed with highly individual and powerful graphics and the use of color

expression in the signage menus and counter front designs."

Specially-designed metal halide up-lighters and low voltage down-lighters combine to give the area a dramatic, yet happy, and well balanced effect.

Solid oak, shaped into organic curves, serve as banquettes and oak slatted metal framed chairs provide the seating. "Emphasis on the wall is created by tiled friezework and the raised circular areas are defined and enclosed by oak balustrades with verdigris finished decorative metal work." Planting is an integral part of the Terrace concept and it includes mounted terra cotta pots off walls, hanging baskets within the ceiling vaults and free standing trees within clover-shaped and circular oak benches.

Design: The John Herbert Partnership, London, England

DINE-O-RAMA FOOD COURT

Gurnee Mills, Chicago, IL

The award-winning Gurnee Mills Food Court takes its inspiration from old cars and America's love affair with automobiles and the open road. The banquettes were custom made to resemble car seats and to further the illusion of being out-of-doors, the ceiling was painted and lit to suggest an evening sky.

To further the imagery even more, the food court tenants' store fronts were designed to be reminiscent of road-side food stands of a by-gone era and these stands are supplemented by suspended "clouds" and "billboards."

There is an overall feeling of "the good old days" — of the '50s and '60s — captured in the design concept — in the motifs and in the colors used to create the Dine-O-Rama food court. It does recall the old time diners — drive-ins and "American Graffiti."

Design: Communication Arts, Boulder, CO
Architect: Cambridge Seven Associates, MA

Design: Communication Arts, Boulder, CO
Arch: Ray Bailey Architects, Houston, TX

EATZ

Santa Monica Place, Santa Monica, CA

The food court was expanded to meet with the new Third St. Promenade and thus form a focal point anchor to the new entertainment mall. Not only did the sign have to attract attention, it also had to serve as a landmark for shoppers trying to find their ways through the center's three levels and four wings. Something about the sign also had to suggest the variety of foods available from the 15 food vendors in the mall.

The all-important sign is constructed of two steel poles which

are connected to the three curving horizontal beams which are, in turn, bolted and welded into steel plates connected to and reinforcing the building's construction. Two of the internally illuminated letters are supported by the poles and the other two are attached to the curving steel bar finished in purple.

The seating area features etched glass railings with cherrywood rails, terrazzo floors and a ceiling trellis. Communication Arts designed all the tenants store fronts thus keeping the overall look homogenous and still each tenant was afforded an individual expression all its own.

TIME-OUT FOOD COURT

Forest Fair Mall, Cincinnati, OH

Under a sweeping, glass filled barrel vaulted skylight and over a black and white checkered floor is the beacon sign that calls "time-out" and invites shoppers from all levels to take some time from their shopping to relax and have something to eat.

The food court incorporates 30 food vendors on two levels and it is anchored by an amusement center. Neon light sculptures, column caps and signage add a festive feeling to the space and spice up the color palette of pale sophisticated neutrals. It is the bold graphics on the floor that helps to organize seating and tenant queuing.

A light cove over the center court — the amusement area — creates a tent-like ceiling and the cove incorporates a computer driven "light graphic" which changes constantly — adding to the show while dining.

Design: Newbold Schkufza, NY
Arch.: Hellmuth, Obata, Kasselbaum, Dallas, TX

BANDSTAND

Franklin Mills, Philadelphia, PA

Franklin Mills is a carnival — a playground — a magic place of light, energy and imagination — and the excitement builds inside the Bandstand theme food court. The Bandstand is a record shop — a diner — a giant juke box — all in one, plus much more.

The main sign is a single giant record platter with neon signage scrawled across it. "Records" are stacked — like in a juke box — beneath it and everything is aglow with the colored lights that emanated from the glorious juke boxes of the '50s and '60s. The giant scale Juke Box combined with the yellow pipe super-structures decorated with more records reappear all over the expansive floor to replay the theme song and play up the joyful mood.

An occasional arch — like a curved music bar spotted with notes, keys and clefs swings over the seating area in keeping with the overall look. The "juke box" design motif is also picked up and re-interpreted in the individual vendor operations that line up on either side of the hall.

Design: Cambridge Seven Associates, MA
Photos: Warren Jagger, Providence, RI

UNIVERSITY MALL FOOD COURT

Carbondale, IL

The 500-seat food court unites the old and new portions of the recently renovated and expanded mall. The space is defined by the high vaulted ceilings with dormers and by the monumentally large windows and dramatic hanging banners that add color and splash to the space.

The edge of the space is marked off by pairs of 25' tall columns which rest on multi-colored bases. They support the exposed roof trusses. To "humanize" the scale of the space it is enriched with landscaping, benches, built-in seating and tables.

To personalize the 7000 sq. ft. space, the designers commission murals that promote the locally-produced foods and these murals are located above the recessed food stands and just below the large windows that fill the court with light. David Peterhans, a principal in Peterhansea — the creators of the murals said, "More than just decoration, environmental graphics such as these provide an image that architecture alone cannot. They communicate, on a human scale, experiences and images that people can relate to — to have fun enjoying."

To Anthony Belluschi, the architects, "The food court works as a uniting factor at a time when the automobile has separated the community." The food court does pay tribute to the community.

Design: Anthony Belluschi, Architects, Chicago, IL

FOOD COURT, MERCHANDISE MART

Chicago, IL

The 18,000 sq. ft. court seats 400 patrons and features eight food vendors. The food court is located on the second level of The Shops at The Mart and it was designed to enhance the Art Deco character of the original building — without necessarily imitating it. "The modern materials and details subtly capture the unique qualities of the Art Deco design, such as linear ornamentation, contrasts of light and dark, geometric patterning and the use of textured glass." The result is warm and inviting with wood used on the ceiling — with custom-made banquettes carrying multi-colored fabric backs, marble tables and wood chairs. To define the entrance and mall frontage, a series of angular glass canopies were incorporated into the design. To bring the people up to the second level, a large abstract hanging element increases the food courts' visibility from the Mart's entrance below.

"The food court is designed to be an attractive gathering place for shoppers and many design oriented employees and visitors to the showrooms located in the Merchandise Mart."

Design: Anthony Belluschi Architects, Chicago, IL
Project Designer: Michael J. Sullivan

CHOICES

There is a whole world that runs on for miles and miles beneath the busy trafficked streets of downtown Toronto and the design firm was asked to renovate the 8000 sq. ft. basement space into a quality fast food court to service the neighborhood office community. This area links up with the underground pedestrian network that thrives below ground level.

One of the major problems facing the designers was the irregular shape of the space and another was the limited ceiling height afforded. By creating a "O" shaped space for the food unit they were able to arrange the irregular shape and the resulting traffic flow was identified by emphasizing the floor pattern which connects to a curved staircase with direct access to street level. Incorporating the skylight from the street level affects "a high volume focal point with natural light." The mechanical obstructions in the ceiling were camouflaged by the multi-level ceiling pattern.

To appeal to the upmarket clientele, the designers selected an Art Deco concept and a palette of warm white, soft green, gray and purple. They used quality materials such as marble, back painted glass, stainless steel, wood and terrazzo — all enhanced by the incandescent light.

This convenient and compact food court offers diners in downtown Toronto an alternative to the usual type service restaurants with no loss of "class."

Design: International Design Group, Toronto, Ontario

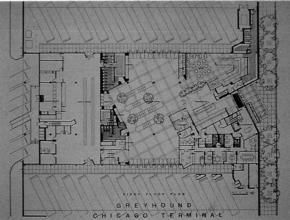

FOOD COURT, GREYHOUND BUS TERMINAL

W. Harrison St., Chicago, IL

Too often we associate the concept of food courts only with malls and shopping centers. With Choices and Merchandise Mart we showed food courts that effectively operate in business buildings and in an earlier chapter we presented some "food court" concepts in airport terminals. This food court is located in the newly constructed Greyhound Bus Terminal in downtown Chicago. It is located off the skylit ticketing lobby and near the two-story high landscaped lounge.

The area is recessed under a dark painted ceiling with a metal grid criss crossing over it. Halide lamps, suspended from the ceiling, illuminate the seating area. The floor is paved in ceramic tiles of two shades of gray and the structural columns are finished in high gloss black. The tables and light metal mesh chairs are all secured to the tile floor and gray concrete planters filled with live foliage serve as a barrier/divider along one open wall.

The bright illumination is reserved for the angled food service counters at the far end of the space which is aglow with the hot pink soffit over the counter and the sizzling neon signage superimposed over it. The counter itself is faced with black and white tiles — set in horizontal bands — and accented with red.

"They get a high level of use on almost a 24-hour schedule calling for hard surfaces that are easy to clean. Still we wanted to create as pleasant an interior as we could." The secured tables and chairs, the plastic laminates, metal fixtures and furniture — all make maintenance simple and the court is always neat and ready to accept travelers who have to wait.

Design: Nagle, Hartray & Associates Ltd., Chicago, IL
Photo: Hedrich Blessing

CENTER COURT FOOD COURT

Madison Square Garden, New York, NY

What would a sporting event be without fast foods? And when they won't bring it to you — you've got to go and get it. However, nobody wants to spend lots of time below when the action is going on in the court or arena above. The food court concept is a natural in sports and theatrical event arenas.

When Communication Arts was called upon to redesign the Madison Square Garden, included in the renovation and modernization program was this food court, two restaurants, and concession stands. Communication Arts designed the graphics for the floor design that decorates the curved sweep of space which is illuminated by halide lamps recessed in the low ceiling. Tall pedestal tables are set about on the terrazzo floor which is rendered in several shades of gray. The designers were also responsible for the back-lit signs that advertise each of the food concession stands including Love Fries, All Star Burgers and Power Play Pizza.

The concessions follow in the same sweep with yellow pipe dividers suggesting separations as well as places for queuing up for service. In comparison to the rest of the space, the service counters and kitchen areas are brilliantly lit with incandescent spots and floods. The mirrored ceiling of the bulkhead that swings across in front of the serving line reflects the color and light of the signage.

Design: Communication Arts, Boulder, CO
Arch: Ellerbe Becket, Kansas City, MO
Photos: Greg Hursley

FOOD COURT AT ROCKINGHAM PARK

Salem, NH

The Mall at Rockingham Park is a super regional shopping center; New Hampshire's largest mall. With three anchors, it boasts some 135 specialty shops and retailers.

This two-story mall features a skylit central concourse with three dramatic courts. The center court, a large rotunda with sweeping grand stair, takes on a new life in the evening with colorful bands of neon and thousands of colorful lights. The center court is adorned with garlands of regional flowers, while stylized horses and jockeys fly across the anchor store courts. The food court is festooned with blue ribbons and fanciful carousel ponies.

The mall has the appearance of a sophisticated suburban mall with race track themes in its decor. The building design does not mimic the look of the nearby racetrack, rather it takes its own artistic stance. Entry canopies of luminous fabric stretched over gracefully curved ironwork frames are reminiscent of Victorian style pavilions. Visible from a distance, they extend the entrance out to the edge of the project's parking structure.

The mall's racing metaphor is carried out in the whimsical use of carousel images. Fanciful horses and fruit done in colors of jockey silks decorate a track around the center's top perimeter. Neon moves in waves reminiscent of carousel decoration. Brightly colored race track-type banners decorated with wildflowers are visible throughout the mall.

Developer/Owner: New England Development, Newton, MA
Architect/Designer: Arrowstreet, Inc., Somerville, MA

FARMER'S MARKETS, GOURMET FOOD /

HEALTH FOOD MARKETS AND MARKETPLACES

"Each night Rome's food came rumbling in on wagons through a fine cobweb of roads; fish caught from the gulfs and the bays, abundant game from the forest, meat and milk from the flocks and herds in the open country. Cheeses, oil, vegetables of every sort; cabbages, lentils, beans and lettuces, radishes and turnips, gourds and pumpkins thundered through the marrow labrinth of streets to the market."

"Consuming Passions," Philippa Pullar

Design: Boyd Associates, Montclair, NJ
Developer: Williams, Jackson, Ewing-Ken Kauffman,
Baltimore, MD

ARDMORE FARMER'S MARKET

Ardmore, PA

Originally the space was a 1930-ish art deco movie house but with the effective rehabbing by Boyd Associates, the 6,388 sq. ft. area is now a neo-traditional Farmers' Market with 12 individual food stalls operated by Amish and Mennonite families — as well as other independent food merchants. Before this current re-design, the space was used as a market — but a market in trouble with the local health department. They were unhappy about the cleanliness and maintenance of the fixtures. While there was a need to up-grade the market, it was equally important to "maintain the vitality and character of the market." Many meetings were held with the merchants, particularly with the Amish, to arrive at a design that they felt comfortable with and that would be acceptable to the traditional Amish values.

Previously established high walls were removed to visually open up the space. Patterns of old plough seats were the basis of the designs used for the perforated and embossed counter skirts around the new modular, stainless steel front and back counters. These fixtures were designed to be easily movable for cleaning and flexible enough to take a variety of sneeze guards and display step configurations.

The space is white and light with white wall tiles and minimal accents — in respect for the Amish preference for simplicity. The painted wood and metal signage was hand lettered by an Amish craftsman and the signage serves as a "counterpoint to the metal fixtures and as a frame for the merchandise along the back wall of each stall." New lighting was also installed to accent the displays and the existing but restored marble floor.

The result is a market for "today's" customer with "traditional values"; plain but striking enough to catch the shopper's fancy.

PIKE'S PLACE MARKET

Seattle, WA

A visit to Seattle isn't a visit to Seattle without a stop to see, smell, taste — and shop the old Pike's Place Market down near the waterfront. It is filled with food gushing out and over-spilling onto the sidewalks that surround this labyrinth of stalls and selling spaces and there is the cacophony of sounds and the spiels of vendors hawking their wares. Fish is the specialty of the market scene and salmon — smoked or fresh — is the big attraction. In addition there are fruits and vegetables — breads and cakes — jams, jellies and all sorts of domestic and imported delicacies. What light there is in the dark, multi-level market is saved to accentuate and highlight the foods and the warm incandescent spots to bring out the rich colors and the sparkle and glisten of fresh fish and produce resting on beds of ice or misted with dew.

The market, located on Pike St. and 1st Ave., was first opened as a farmers market in 1907 and today it is a complex — a warren of retail hutches — that includes — in addition to the food products — arts and crafts shops, wandering minstrels and street artists, assorted shops and novelty stores as well as an assortment of cafes and restaurants for those who can't wait to try the specialties of the market.

Photos: MMP/RVC

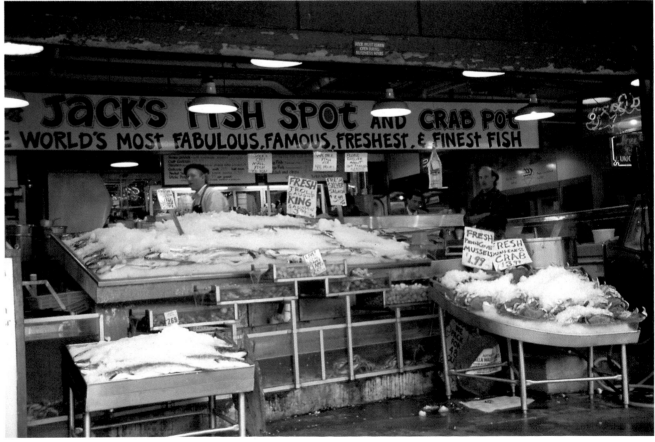

PUBLIC MARKET

Granville Island, Vancouver, BC

Like the Pike's Place Market, a visit to Granville Island — a reclaimed industrial area — is a "must" for anybody visiting Vancouver. It is a delightful five-to-ten minute boat/taxi away — but a trip well worth making. In addition to the arts and crafts shops and boutiques, restaurants and cafes, fashion stores, experimental theaters and cabarets, the island features a giant shed that houses the Public Market; a farmers market par excellence. The vast, skylit interior is filled with produce and prepared foods, specialty shops, and even a food court for those who want to enjoy an "eat in" — as well as a "take-out." The market isn't big on "decor" nor is it beautifully fixtured or handsomely signed, but it is alive and exciting and filled to overflowing with color. The visitor can travel the cement aisles following his/her eyes —or nose — since the smells of spices, prepared foods, freshly baked goodies and coffee roasting or brewing serve as directionals around the space.

The AAA Tour book describes it as follows: "Seafood, especially salmon, and an accompanying abundance of fresh fruits and vegetables are the culinary basis of Vancouver's restaurants. A vivid example of the city's cornucopia is the Granville Island market where displays of fresh salmon, black cod and other seafood delicacies are set amid stalls of Okanagan fruits and fresh flowers."

Photos: MMP/RVC

MERCADO LIBERDAD

Guadalajara, Mexico

Imagine a giant concrete and cement structure that encompasses several square blocks. Imagine three floors crammed full of shops and stalls — kiosks and kitchens — all surrounding a vast open central court which is already stuffed tight with vendors and displays of fruits, vegetables, and flowers — of breads and cakes — candies, nuts and sticky sweets. Imagine a spectrum of color gone amok — a rampage on the senses — an attack upon the eyes — the nose — the ears. That is only the beginning of what the Mercado Liberdad in Guadalajara is all about. Tourists are rarely seen here; this is a local affair though the market draws its vendors and its customers from the countryside all around the city. On the four sides of this mammoth construction and on all of its levels there are shops featuring arts and crafts, novelties, china, glass, cookware, clothing, records, tapes and even videos. An occasional visitor (non-local) may find his/her way into the cavernous hall only to be swept up by the throng of humanity — swept up the ramps that connect the many levels of the market.

A major part of the second level is devoted to "eat-in" shops; to fast food operations that consist of open preparation areas surrounded on four sides by old laminate counters polka-dotted with sundry, unmatched stools. As a come-on, samples of the specialty of "the house" are displayed under bare bulbs dangling off electric cords. The "display" can be a grinning goat's skull in a bed of foliage and garlanded with peppers, onions and tamales, but featured it is — instead of a sign board.

Photos: MMP/RVC

MAUNAKEA MARKETPLACE

Honolulu, HI

This farmers market is located in the Chinese section of Honolulu surrounded by noted and non-noted Chinese restaurants, decorative imported arts stores and food specialty shops. The market is located adjacent to a community center in a bi-level structure and it was designed to appeal to the all important Asian community as well as the Caucasian shoppers who come here for produce they can't find in other markets.

The cement paved floors hold the painted wood floor fixtures colored in beige and accented with bright blue. The same blue frames the cut out red lacquered signs that hang overhead and are lettered in yellow. Fluorescent lamps are suspended down from the high raftered ceiling and spotlights accent and enhance the fresh produce and food products spread out with a show of abundance. Raised up on a mezzanine, near the entrance, is a small but pleasant arrangement of tables and chairs for those who prefer to eat what they have just purchased rather than bring it home.

The market's signage, the controlled look of the floor fixtures and the lighting make this farmers' market appear more upscaled — and not quite as exotic as one would expect to see in this old historic ethnic area. The rice and spice shops around it more than make up for it by being truly "picturesque."

Photos: MMP/RVC

BELK STORE

Greensboro, NC and Winston Salem, NC

Southpark, Charlotte, NC

The Belk Department Stores pay special attention to their Food Halls. Usually they are located on the lowest level — near cookware and the china departments. The food departments feature delicacies and gift items and packages as well as prepared foods — to go. Natural wood and white — white ceramic tiles and natural wood laid floors make up the signature elements of the area usually accented with sharp black and maybe a spot of red. Lots of warm and pleasant incandescent lamps are used to add a "home and hearth" feeling to the retail space. Wall cabinets and refrigerated cases carry their own tubular fluorescent strip lighting.

In the two Schafer Associates designed shops on p.221 the black and white checkerboard pattern plays an important part in the natural wood and white fixtured shop. No Belk Food Hall would be complete without a coffee shop or cafe — a small seating area where tired shoppers can sit at ease with a cup of coffee and sample some of the freshly baked goods available in that department.

Design: Schafer Assoc., Oakbrook Terrace, IL
Photos: MMP/RVC

SUTTON PLACE GOURMET

Woodholme S/C, Baltimore, MD

This 14,000 sq. ft. store anchors the Festival at Woodholme S/C in an affluent suburb of Baltimore. Like the other full service Sutton Place Gourmet stores in the Washington, DC and Arlington, VA area, this store features a complete, carefully merchandised and beautifully presented array of delicious prepared foods, fresh ingredients and packaged goods.

The color scheme is simple but emphatic; it is basically white and tan with crisp accents of black and highlights of bright red. This allows the full focus to remain on the abundant and appealing — and beautifully lit — displays of fresh produce, meats, seafood and hearth baked breads. The signage is sharp and consistent in white on black panels, and the red reappears on the lamp shades that hang down over the counters and the occasional tent top that floats over a skirted feature table out near the aisle. High tech wire and perforated metal gondolas support the packaged goods while straw and rattan baskets and the aforementioned tablecloths "soften" the effect on the selling floor. They add gracious, homey decorative notes.

The ceiling is patterned with recessed fluorescent luminaires that provide the light ambience to the already white space and the metal shaded drop lights and the white spotlight cannisters on the ceiling mounted tracks combine to accentuate the rich and warm colors of the prepared foods and produce.

A companion cafe opens into the store and it adds "color and a friendly bustle that sets the tone for the hospitable ambience of the store." This store is already an outstanding success in this location; it gives the shoppers what they want — and what they have come to expect from the Sutton Place Gourmet operation.

Design: Mark Ksiazewski, Dir. of Facilities Design
Photos: Rich Larson

OVER THE COUNTER

Park Ave., New York, NY

This sophisticated gourmet shop not only carries prepared foods to take out but also an array of fine packaged foods — all handsomely arranged and displayed in the long, narrow midtown store. The very high ceiling is painted a cerulean blue and only the Corinthian capped piers are allowed to travel way up into the blue to meet the 19' ceiling. The 1100 sq. ft. shop appears warmer and more intimate due to the hand painted/stenciled "tile" pattern on the walls in beiges and grays. Standing before them are pine wood cabinets that have been white washed in a pastel beige and trimmed with deep crown moldings. White milk glass lamps, based on a design of a bye-gone era extend down from the ceiling to bring a flattering light onto the products on display. The natural terra cotta tiled floor is patterned with decorative tiles to complete the Tuscany inspired design scheme.

Using old weathered crates, beaten and scarred provincial style tables and country artifacts as display props and elevations, the Italian-style food shop presents its pastas, pasta sauces, olives and olive oils, sacks of rice, boxes of imported biscuits, syrups and fruit preserves, coffee, teas and even freshly baked breads.

Design: Haverson Rockwell Architects, PC, New York, NY
Partner in Charge: Jay M. Haverson
Decorative Painter: Tom Perta, Artist Representative
Photos: Kloubes/Rogers-Heliostudio, New York, NY

PUSATERI'S FINE FOODS

Toronto, Ontario, Canada

This is a new addition to an existing and successful supermarket in Toronto. In redesigning the existing space and the add-on, the designers attempted to "create a semi-traditional environment which would give a high quality feel to the merchandise." To achieve that upscaled look and to give even greater emphasis to the "Fine Foods" in the store's name, the area was divided into smaller selling spaces and "shops" and "boutiques" were formed to affect a sense of intimacy.

The color scheme is basically white accented with grayed down teal and surrounded with lots of natural woods and textures. The floors are white ceramic tiles laid in a grid pattern — or in an over-scaled brick design. Natural wood trellises hang down from the white ceiling and they are caught up in vines, entwined with branches and dried foliage, and hung with straw and wicker baskets and provincial cookware. The baked goods counter combines vertical granite strips with horizontal bands of stainless steel and copper. The wall cabinets and the standing floor fixtures — also looking like cupboards — are constructed on ruddy colored wood and trimmed with teal.

In the meat department, red tiles are used to accent the all white shop and red metal lamp shades bring the incandescent lamps down to show off the meat in the counters. Overhead the wood trellis is laden with dried foliage and copper cook pans.

The produce counters are painted deep teal/green and bordered and outlined with red. Hanging plants "warm" this area with its teal walls and white floors.

Design: Candeloro Design Group, Pat Candeloro
Architect: Gabor & Popper, Architects

CUCINA RUSTICA

Columbus Ave., New York, NY

Cucina Rustica is a neighborhood store that is much more than it first seems to be — though the prolific presentation of packaged goods in the turquoise painted storefront is the first indication that something special goes on in there. This long, tall, narrow store is only one door down from a charming little Italian restaurant that is also owned and operated by the Rebracas. This is a store that could be considered, by some, cliche and kitsch — if it weren't for the love and affection and the exquisite presentation of the prepared foods and packaged foods that are squeezed into every available inch of this old store. Antiques and artifacts — related and unrelated — share the cramped space with the weathered wood counters and fixtures — with the wicker baskets that usurp what little walking space there is left on the country-style, terra cotta tiled floor.

The "aged' and "stained" walls are overwhelmed with portraits of "family" — of the "old country" — all done tongue-in-cheek to the delight of the knowing and sophisticated shoppers who live and shop on Columbus Ave. They recognize the array of prepared foods presented with wild abandon and in abundance as gourmet delights — and they relish their purchases as much as their visits to the shop.

Up front, near the entrance, the "moderne" fixture, circa 1950, shows off a great selection of baked goods and it is another incongruous note in the stimulating interior. Behind it is a selection of coffees-to-go and during the day there is a steady stream, in and out of Cucina Rustica, of pedestrians carrying their "coffee and" selected from the breads, cakes, pastries and muffins all on display. No coffee goes out alone!

Design: Nick & Patricia Rebraca, owners
Photos: MMP/RVC

PANCONE ITALIAN SPECIALTY STORE

Bradley Beach, NJ

When an architect of markets who lives almost 100 miles away and who had nothing whatsoever to do with the store's design or layout says, "You have to see Pancone's —you'll want it for your book," — you go look. We looked and we had it photographed because for over 40 years this Italian Specialty Store has been growing and growing — ever expanding — and in an area that really hasn't seen that much growth. Bradley Beach is, however, a beach resort town that more than quadruples its population during the summer months. It is then that the visitors "discover" the wonders to be had in the world of Pancone — and they are never free again. This is an institution and its patrons will return from many miles away to shop the specialities — the prepared foods, the imported staples, and the always fresh breads, cakes and pastries that have added luster to the Pancone name. It is not necessarily the ambience they are coming for, though the several adjoining shops are neat, clean and simply practical. It is the presentation and the abundance of product on view in the spartan white setting that does it.

Small white tiles like the kind we "remember" from our youth in old corner grocery stores or the friendly bar and grill cover the floors banded and patterned with blue. A blue checkerboard pattern also faces some of the counters while other display cases are finished in a bright, sharp blue. This is a "family affair" and the family's history is recorded in aging photographs and clippings in the crisp white walls. Cool blue neon bands outline the ceiling and also provide signage that sparkles. The non-dramatic setting sits back and lets the merchandise take over — yet there is something in the design that suggests "heritage" and "tradition."

What began as a delicatessen in the 1950s has grown to include a bakery, a produce section, and now a cafe has been added to the Pancone phenomenon.

Owners: Ethel & John Pancone
Photos: Louis Bernstein, Springfield, NJ

DANAL PROVISIONS

Bank St., New York, NY

Take an old, high-ceilinged store front in Greenwich Village — chip and chop back to the original rose-colored brick walls that lie underneath; stencil the worn and weary wood floors with a fanciful checkerboard in gentle, muted colors; fixture the space inexpensively with discarded or second-hand tired tables peeling paint, weathered wood crates, barrels, sacks of burlap and an occasional odd wall cabinet or armoire; light the space with incandescent spots and floods encased in old fashioned green metal drop fixtures; decorate and display the natural foods, the produce, the baked goods and the packaged goods with all the skill you have developed over all the years spent in department store display — and what have you got? You have Danal; a delightful stage set for food — eclectic, colorful, warm and friendly — a food shop that says "natural" and "home-made" at first viewing. Even the white refrigerator cases seem to blend in well in this melange of textures and natural, earthy colors as does the white tile faced counter up front that is backed up by coffee cannisters. The owners/designers have a background in visual merchandising — and it shows — and it sells.

Design: San Saltiel & Albert Volk, owners
Photos: MMP/RVC

232

GRASSROOTS NATURAL FOODS & KITCHEN

So. Pasadena, CA

"To create a more open feeling, we lightened the color scheme to Southwestern colors and changed from incandescent lighting to fluorescents." The open feeling was important as was the traffic flow into and through the store — and the designers were also expected to increase the selling space. "Through analysis of traffic flow and destination areas, we were able to ease congestion and aid in the overall shop-ability of the retail establishment."

To provide a sense of direction in this warm peach/beige/pale aqua interior, a floor accent was designed with a three square arrow that creates a subliminal direction pointer. The use of accent colors and the "directional theme" did help to improve the traffic flow in the relatively small space. Colorful graphics, above eye level, add to the fresh feeling of the shop and even the slatwall fixtures of pale beige are accented with color; the light aqua that also appears on the HVAC system that soars overhead. The owners, Meir and Maria Puni, have been delighted with the results and with the effective cost saving change from air conditioning to swamp cooler in the kitchen.

Design: Pacific Store Design, Orange, CA   Chris Miller
Architect: Marty Piatt, AIA

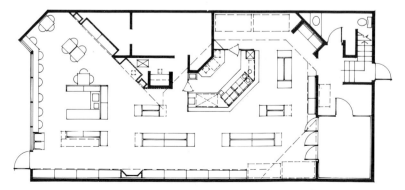

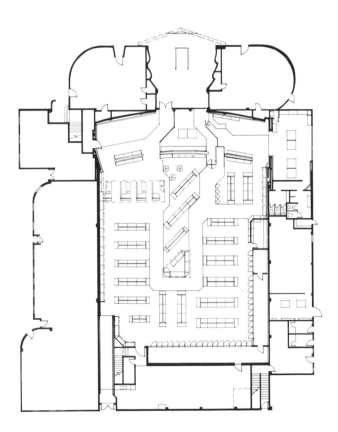

Design: Pacific Store Design, Orange, CA
Design Team: Chris Miller/Jim Rasmus
Photos: Chris Miller

CLARK'S NUTRITION

Riverside, CA

The De Anza movie theater is a landmark building in Riverside and it is now the new home of Clark's Nutrition. "Our goal was to create a bold image that would enhance the store's heavy sports nutrition background." It took some doing considering the age of the building, the sloped floor of the interior and the restrictions brought on by the landmark status.

The walls, floor and laminate fixtures are all white banded and accented with cerulean blue. A theme mural suggesting a positive, healthy image was painted on the fascia above the wall fixtures by a local artist, Jerry Ragg. The concept was that from the top of this building, on a clear day, one could see the local mountains, desert, farms, and even down to the ocean. The artist enlarged each of these landscapes and painted life-size joggers, cyclists, and even body builders, doing their sporty thing.

The all-important bulk food area was given special design attention. Unlike typical bulk bins, these were designed into a walk-in cold box to ensure freshness and lengthen the shelf life. Having the back stock adjacent to these rear-feed gravity bins allows the F.I.F.O. (first in-first out) automatic rotation of all products in this area.

This new store has become a landmark destination for many health-minded shoppers.

EADIE'S KITCHEN & MARKET

Sears Tower, Chicago, IL

Design: Meisel Ltd. Associates, Chicago, IL
Photos: Joe Meisel

How do you get them down on the farm after they've been up in the Tower? Bring them into Eadie's Kitchen and Market — a down-on-the-farm, wholesome old homestead for fine foods to go and for produce to purchase in the midst of all the contemporary styling about it. The tiled floors are pale gray inset with tiles of peach and the walls are painted in bands that ombre from gray to pale aqua to deeper shades of aqua — defined with rails and moldings but even then there is a country casual feeling about the space especially up front with a display of fruits and vegetables in baskets and bushels, and a slate-board on an easel with hand-noted specials of the day chalked on.

Inside, the glass fronted cases are surrounded by grayed aqua panels and the foods are presented within the illuminated units. In another area, snacks are available on high tech, perforated chrome and grid shelf units but the merchandise is displayed — for easy picking — in straw baskets of assorted sizes and shapes and even in old "fire" buckets. The latticed windows look sort of "old fashioned" and the wall beneath the deeper aqua rail is tiled in two tones of gray. Nothing could be less "down on the farm" than the MR16 lamps on the track system attached to the ceiling but the lights certainly make the products and packages come alive in bright, pure color.

JULIAN'S GOURMET MARKET

Monroe Dr., Atlanta, GA

Though located in midtown Atlanta, this 2000 sq. ft. "shoe-box" of a store serves both the in-town and suburban gourmet client. The shop offers unusual cookery baked goods along with an extensive selection of pates and imported cheeses.

"The design is intended to communicate a sense of stability with a nostalgic flavor." In order to accommodate the large selection of merchandise, certain physical changes had to be made including the removal of the drop ceiling tiles and the reduction of the stock room space to a minimum. In the new design, the merchandise is stacked on shelves that go way up to the ceiling and a rolling library ladder goes from one end of the store to the other providing access to the upper shelves.

The cash counter also serves as the check out and the service area for cheese, pate and olives by the pound. A variety of fresh pesto sauces is also on display here. The vertical surfaces are clad in a beaded ash wood stained with a white wash and custom colored ceramic tile pavers top the cash stand and the service counter. The walls and the plastic laminate that is used are a deep clay color "to provide a warm background for the products." The designers also had the decking above the ceiling sprayed a deep forest green so that though the feeling of space is maintained — the HVAC system is theatrically camouflaged.

The lighting plan includes 2X4 drop fluorescent fixtures with chrome para wedge lenses for general illumination and white enameled goose neck lamps are used to accent the changing menu board. A shed roof with fluorescent up-lights defines the area flanking the cash stand and halogen down lights also appear along with "old fashioned" white globe lights in the effective lighting plan.

Design: Landes Design Group, Inc., Atlanta, GA
Photos: Wayne Smith Photography

ABOUT THE EDITOR

Martin M. Pegler has long been considered a
leading authority on store design and visual
merchandising. He has been involved in the field
for almost forty years and has worked in all
phases of merchandise presentation: designer,
manufacturer, display person, store planner and
consultant. Witty, urbane, erudite and most
persuasive, he has long been a vocal champion of
store design and visual presentation as a
necessary and respected part of retailing. This
has made him a popular speaker across the
country and for two tours of the British Isles,
Mexico and Japan. He is in demand as a lecturer
for industry, small business groups as well as,
nation-wide chains and shopping centers.

Mr. Pegler is author of *Successful Food
Merchandising & Display, Stores of the Year,
Store Windows That Sell, Food Presentation &
Display, Home Furnishings Merchandising &
Store Design,* and *Market Supermarket &
Hypermarket Design.*

He is currently a professor of Store Planning and
Visual Merchandising at the Fashion Institute of
Technology in New York and travels extensively,
— always searching the field for new and fresh
approaches, ideas and techniques to share.